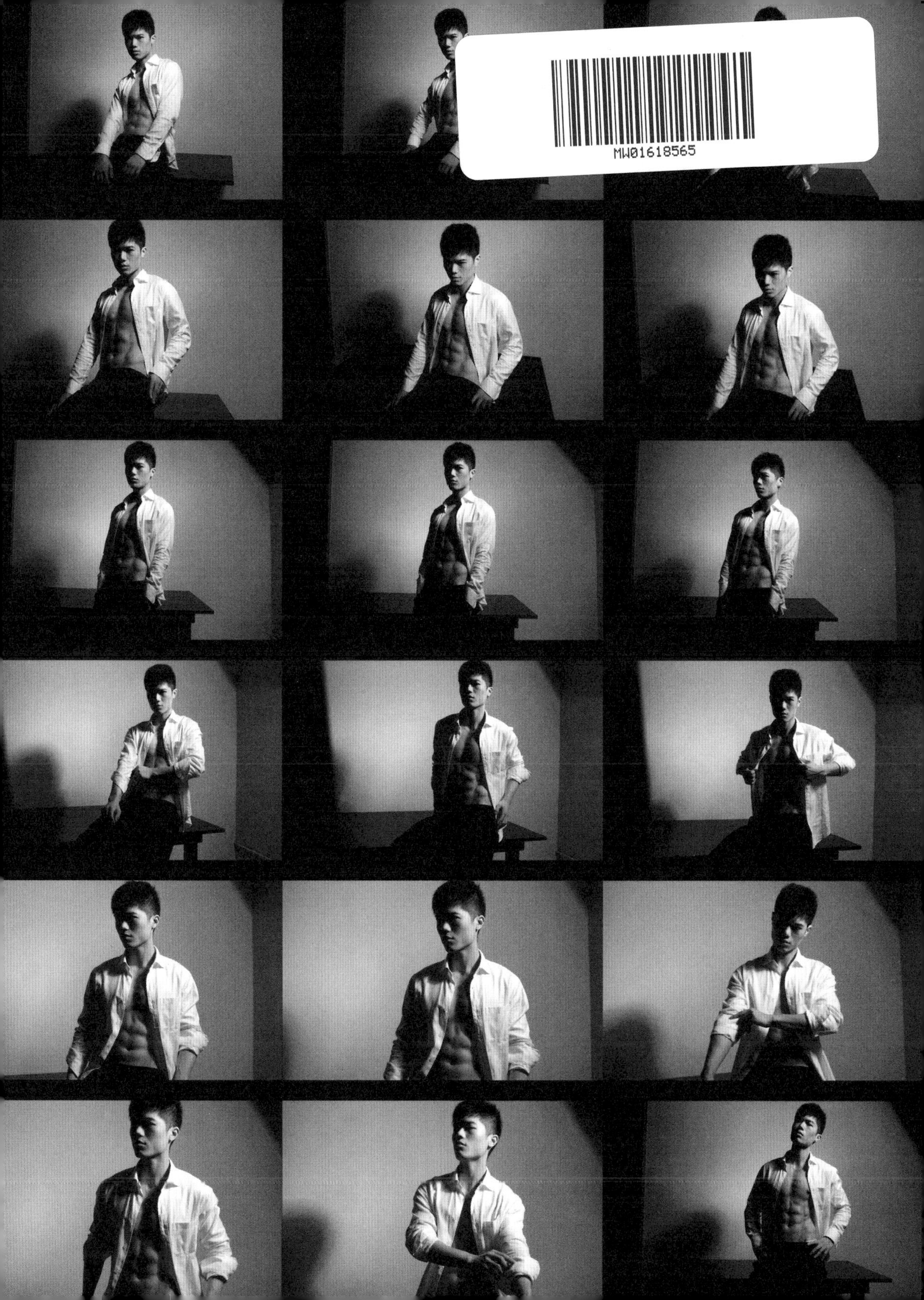

beaux

the asian male magazine

noun (plural beaux or beaus /bəʊz, bəʊ/)

1 a boyfriend or male admirer.
2 a rich, fashionable young man; a dandy.

beauxmagazine.com

Studio 8 Hong Kong Publishing Ltd.
Room 802, Block B
Hong Kong Chai Wan Industrial Building
26 Lee Chung Street
Chai Wan, Hong Kong
T +852 2540 6267
F +852 2542 4208
http://studio8hongkong.com

ISBN 978 988 98259 4 2

body

voice

Printed Matter. Made in Hong Kong.

No words can describe the beauty of these two phrases or the passion I hold for the printed page. Printed matter matters to me. I love the way books and magazines are put together. I love the texture of paper, the various ways in which it interacts with different inks, the lacquered sheen of a finished print, even the way books are bound and secured. All these hold an indescribable fascination to me. On this matter alas, I am no expert. The lovely lady with dark-rimmed glasses who runs that small printing business across the hall from my studio is. And so, to her I listen and I learn.

These are my thoughts. The printed page will never fade away. I believe that the best printed matter will primarily consist of truly fine publications that people will treasure unconditionally. Looking back to a statement I wrote in 2005 for *The Asian Male – 1.AM,* my first publication, my stated goal was to create something tangible, something to hold, to flip through with your fingers, page by page. No swiping. No pinching. There can be no true replacement for the tactile world of actual print; of seeing a photograph not only with your sight but also by your touch.

The theme to V1 (Volume 1) of **beaux** is vanity. Once a reserved privilege for the Asian female, vanity now finds itself beholden to the Asian male. The photography in **beaux** magazine embraces this shift; we celebrate this progression as a natural evolution in culture. I hope you will enjoy this issue of **beaux** as much as I did building it. I hope this hybrid book/ magazine will continue to grow and flourish and I hope to achieve this with like-minded photographers, art-lovers and Asian male admirers.

Norm Yip
Founder and Publisher

FOLIO 1

by Norm Yip

The photographs showcased in the ***folio*** *section are available for sale as signed limited edition prints. For more information, contact us at* ***enquiry@beauxmagazine.com****.*

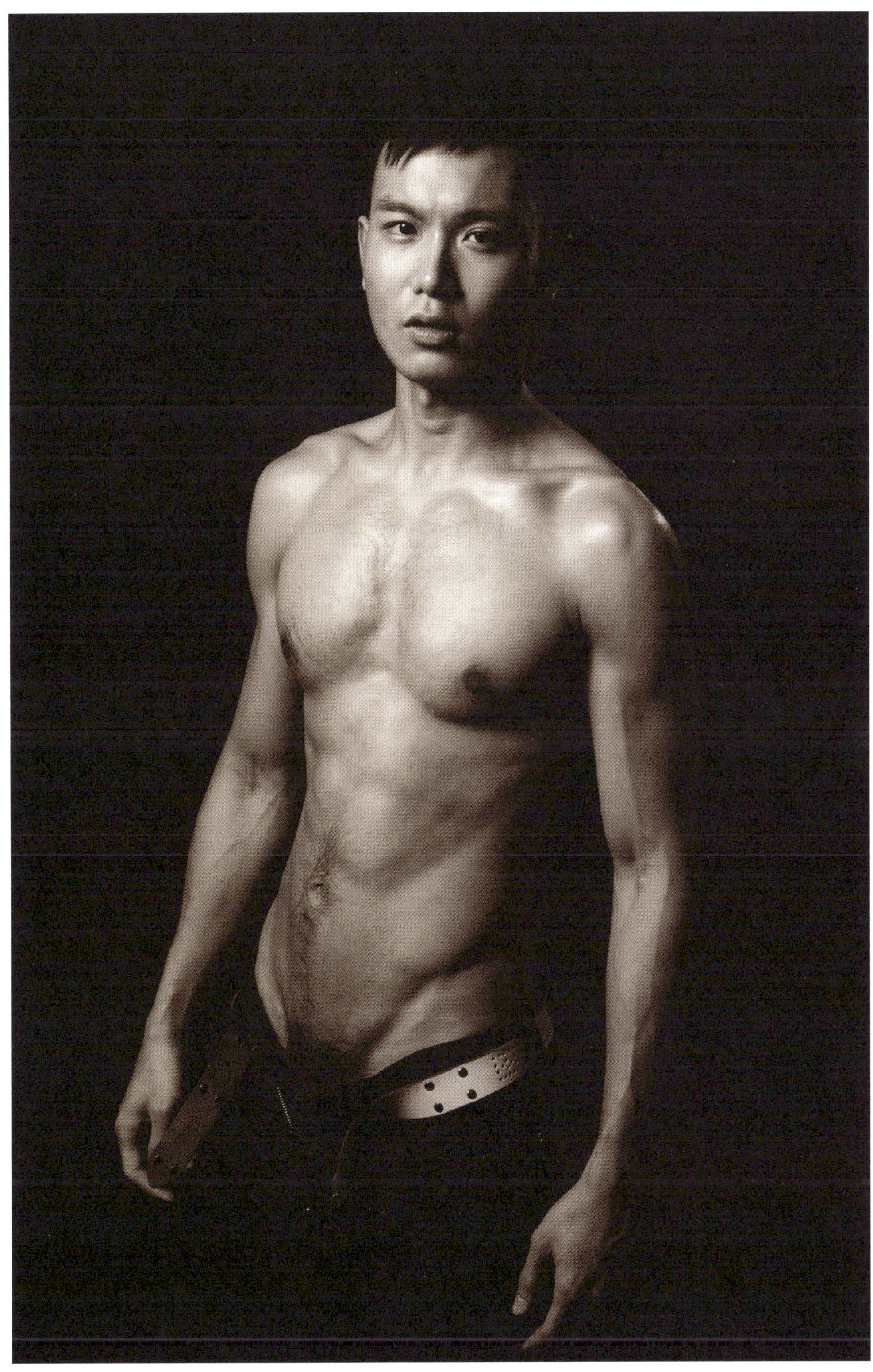

Loren Tam, Chinese, Hong Kong

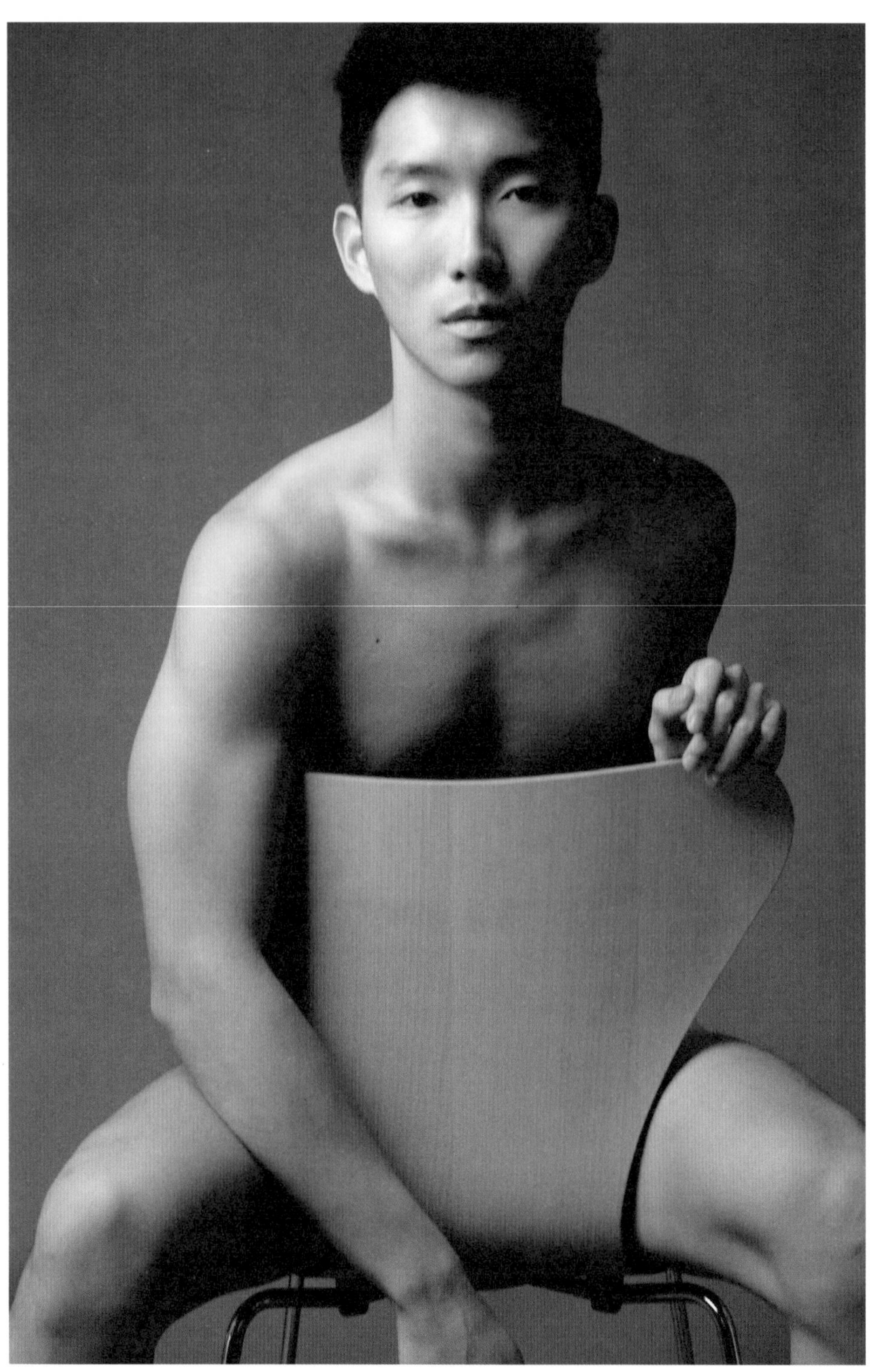

John Yip, Chinese, Hong Kong

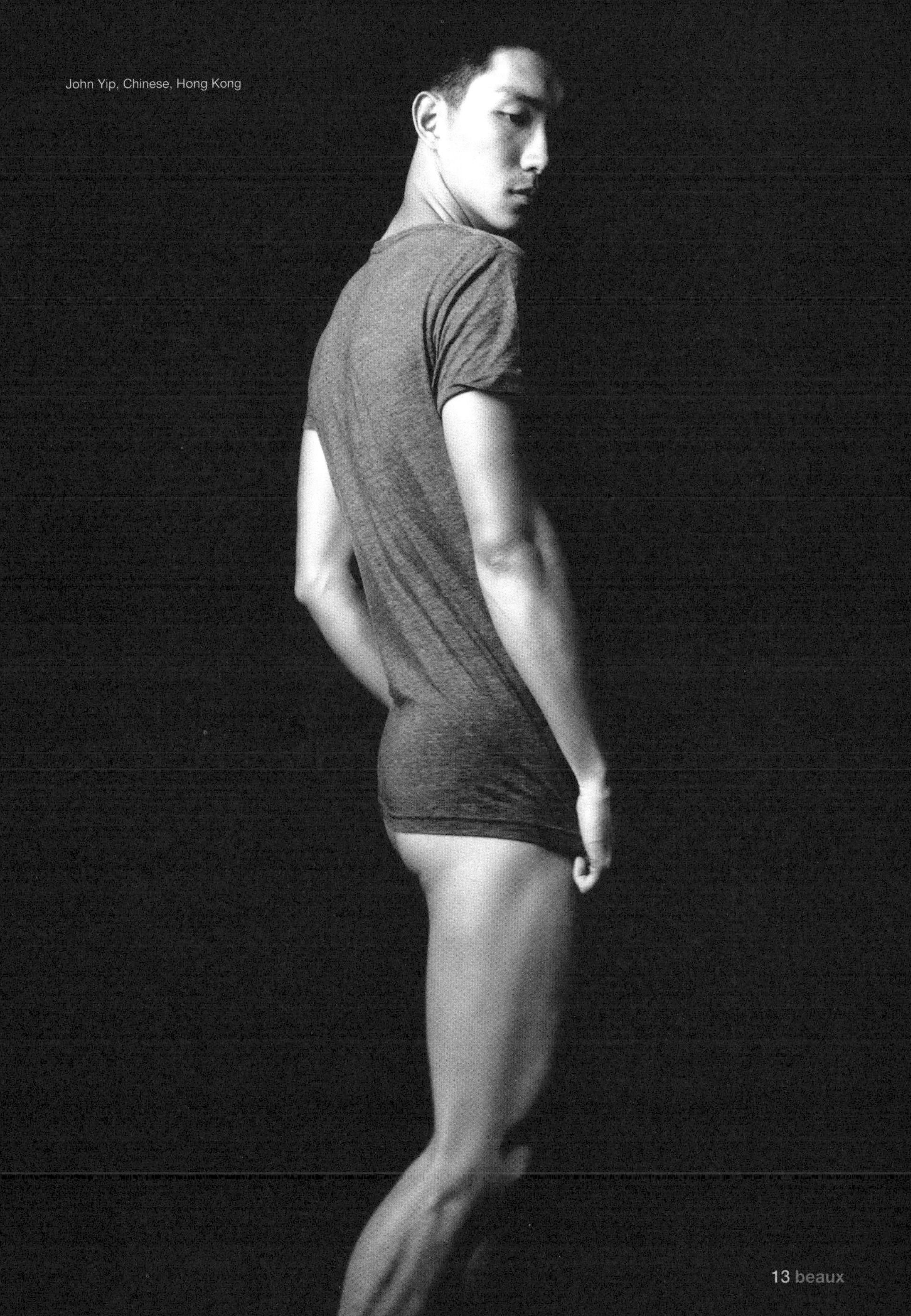

John Yip, Chinese, Hong Kong

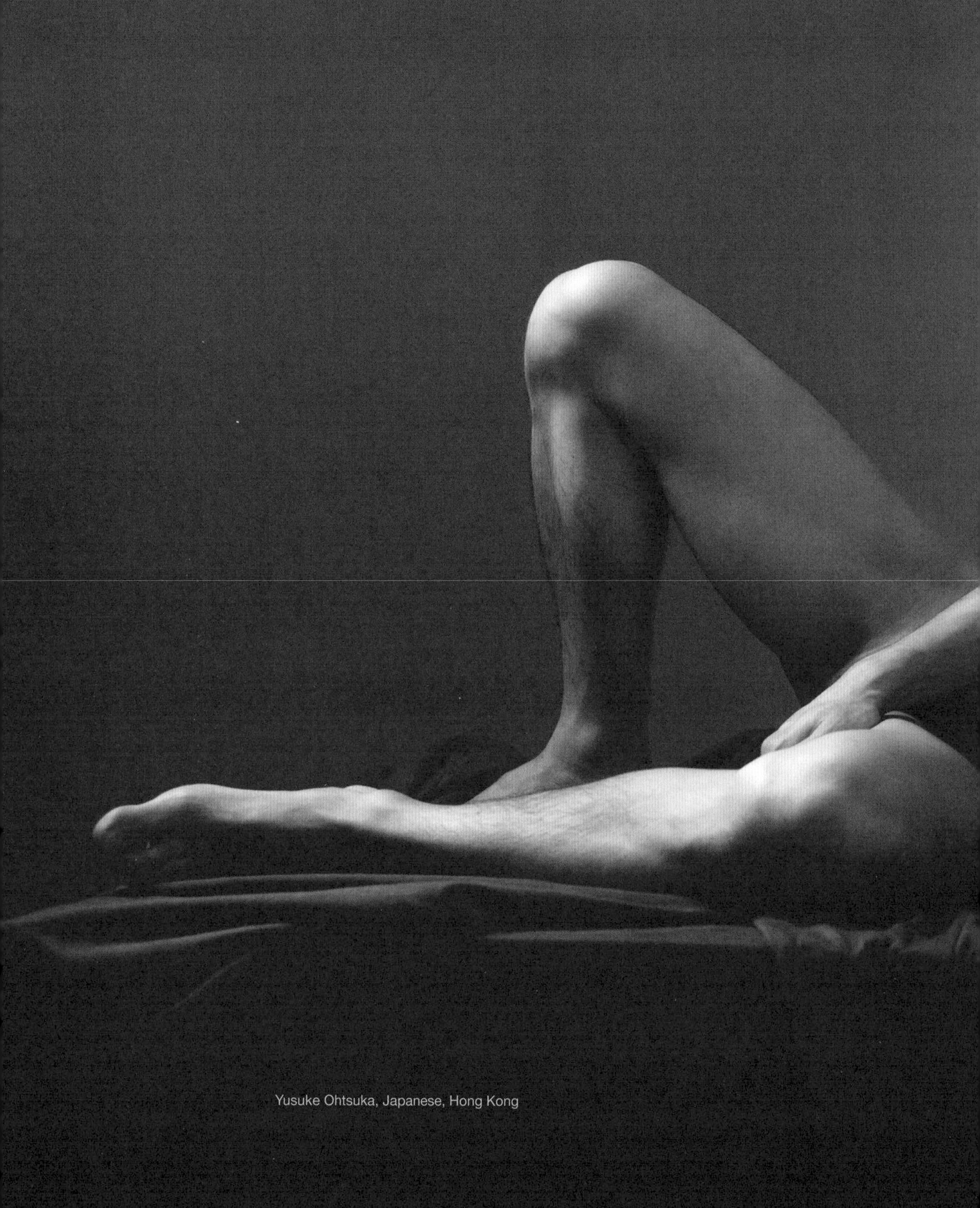

Yusuke Ohtsuka, Japanese, Hong Kong

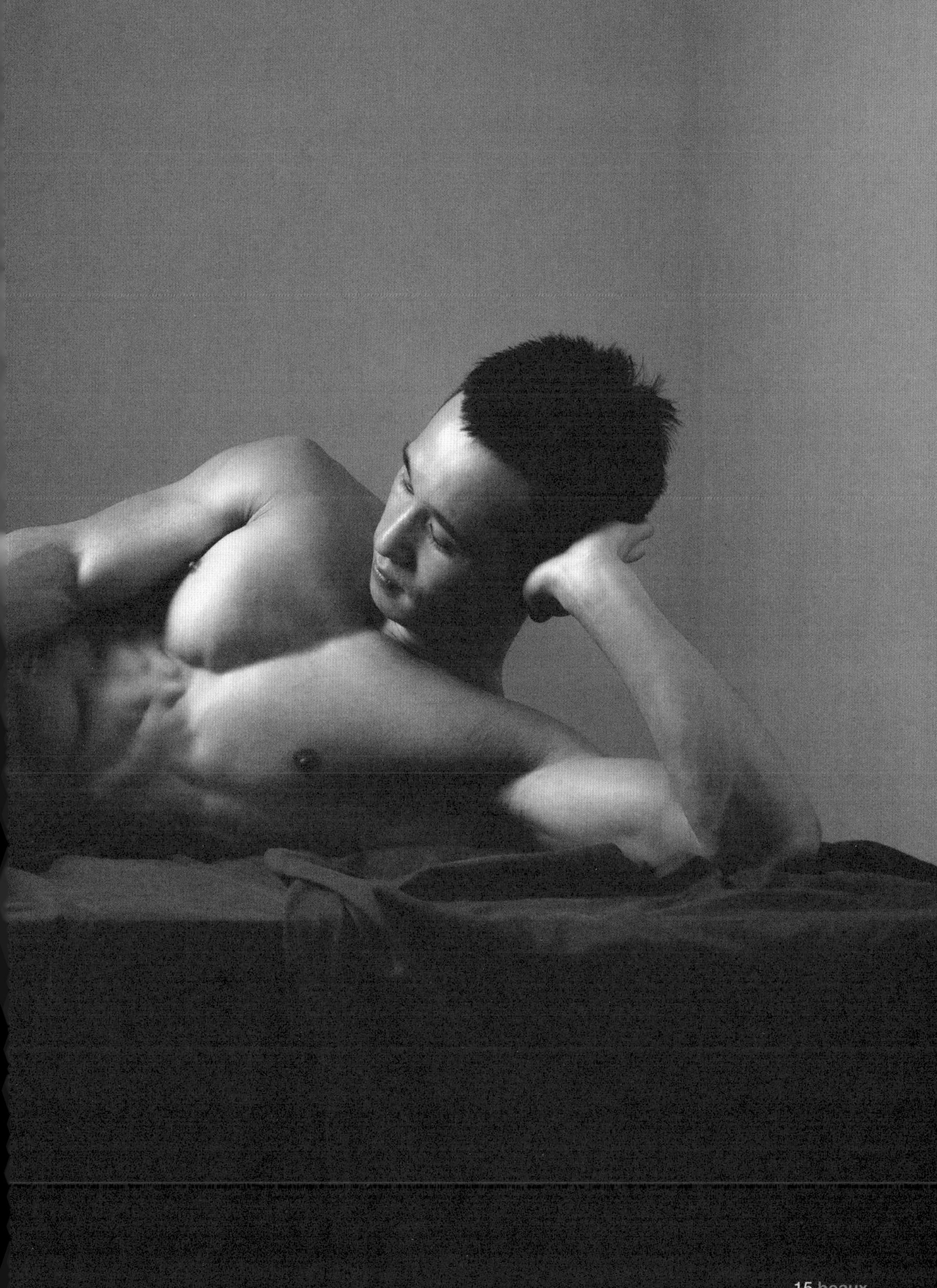

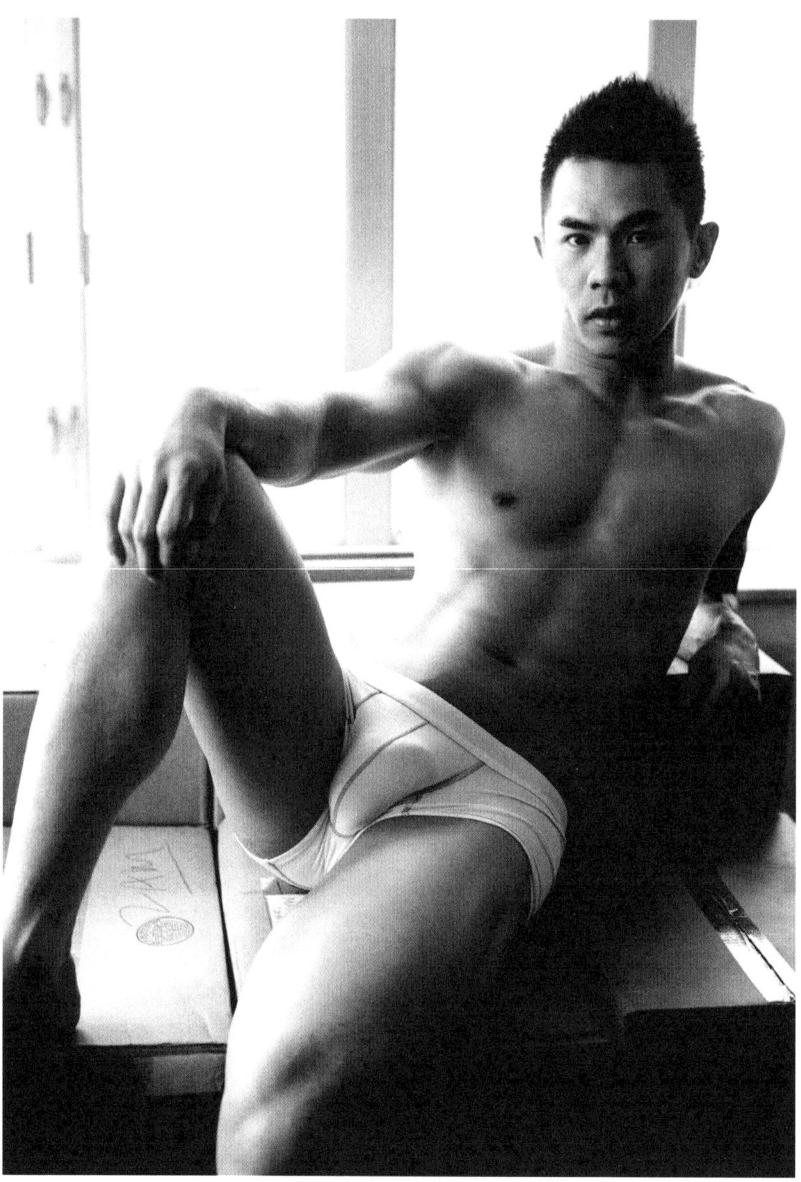

Joe Wong, Chinese, Malaysia

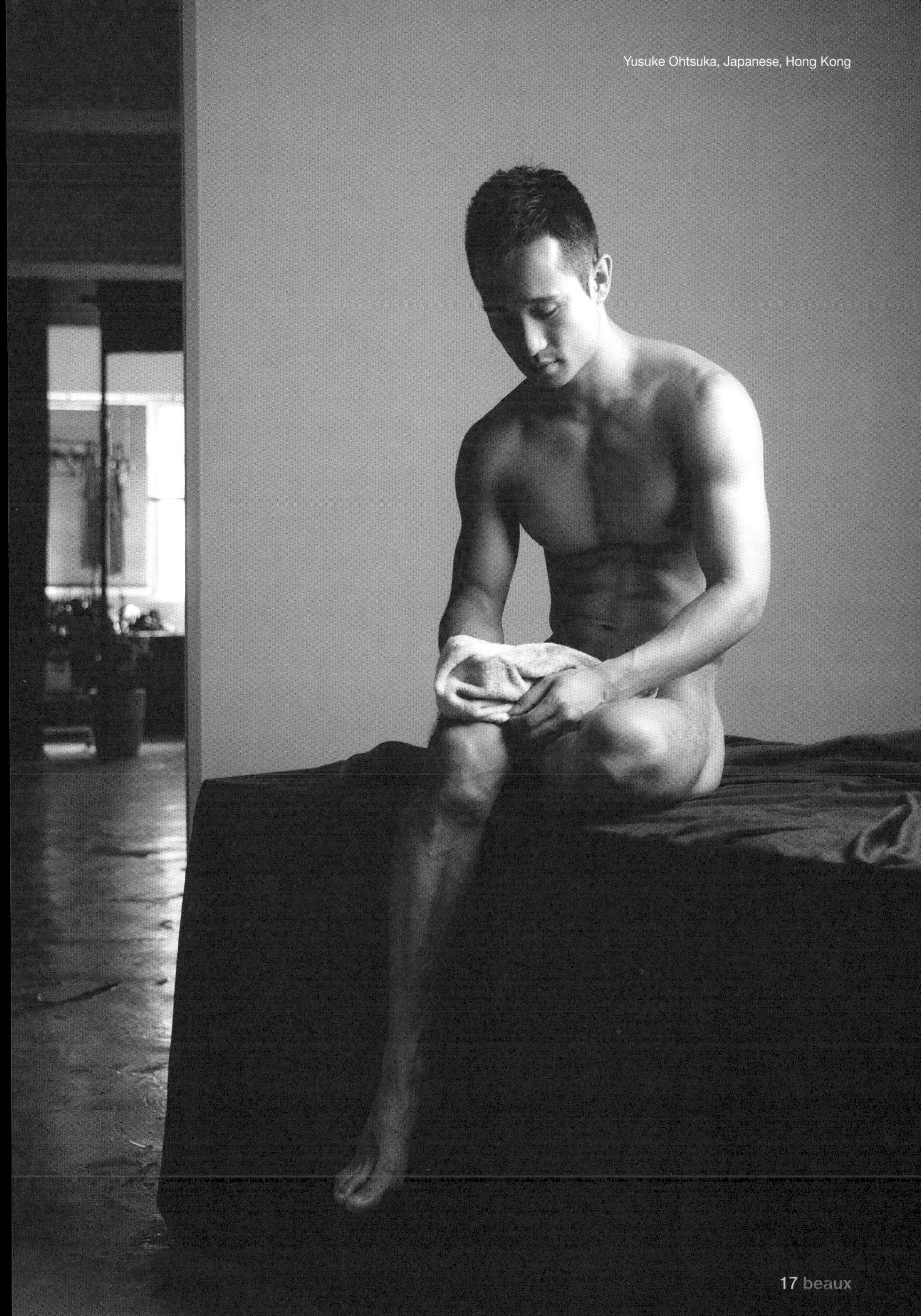

Yusuke Ohtsuka, Japanese, Hong Kong

shootout 1

Photographer Norm Yip
Model Derek Cheong, Chinese, Malaysia
Styling Patryk Chaou
Makeup Jimmy Chung
Location Studio 8

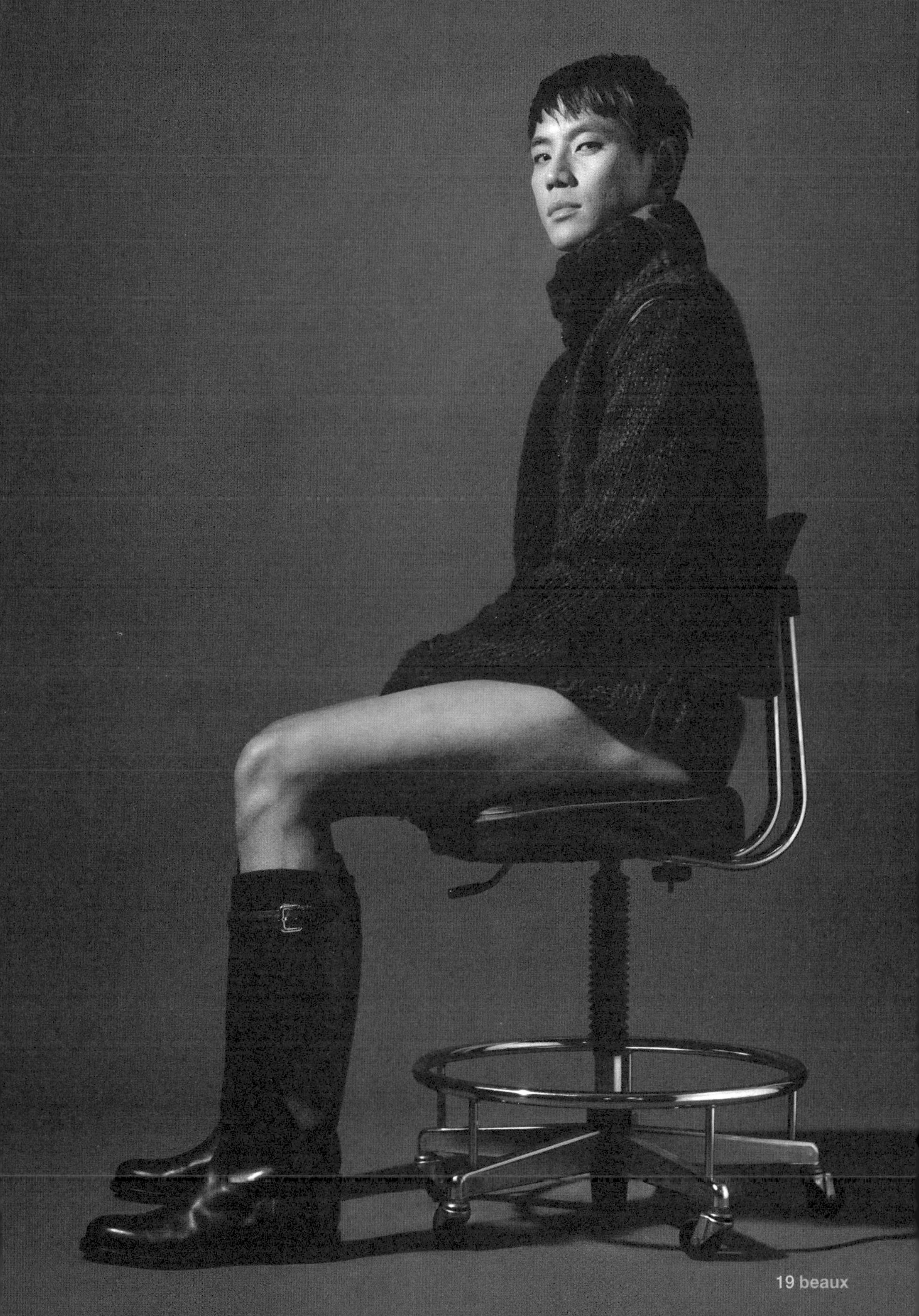

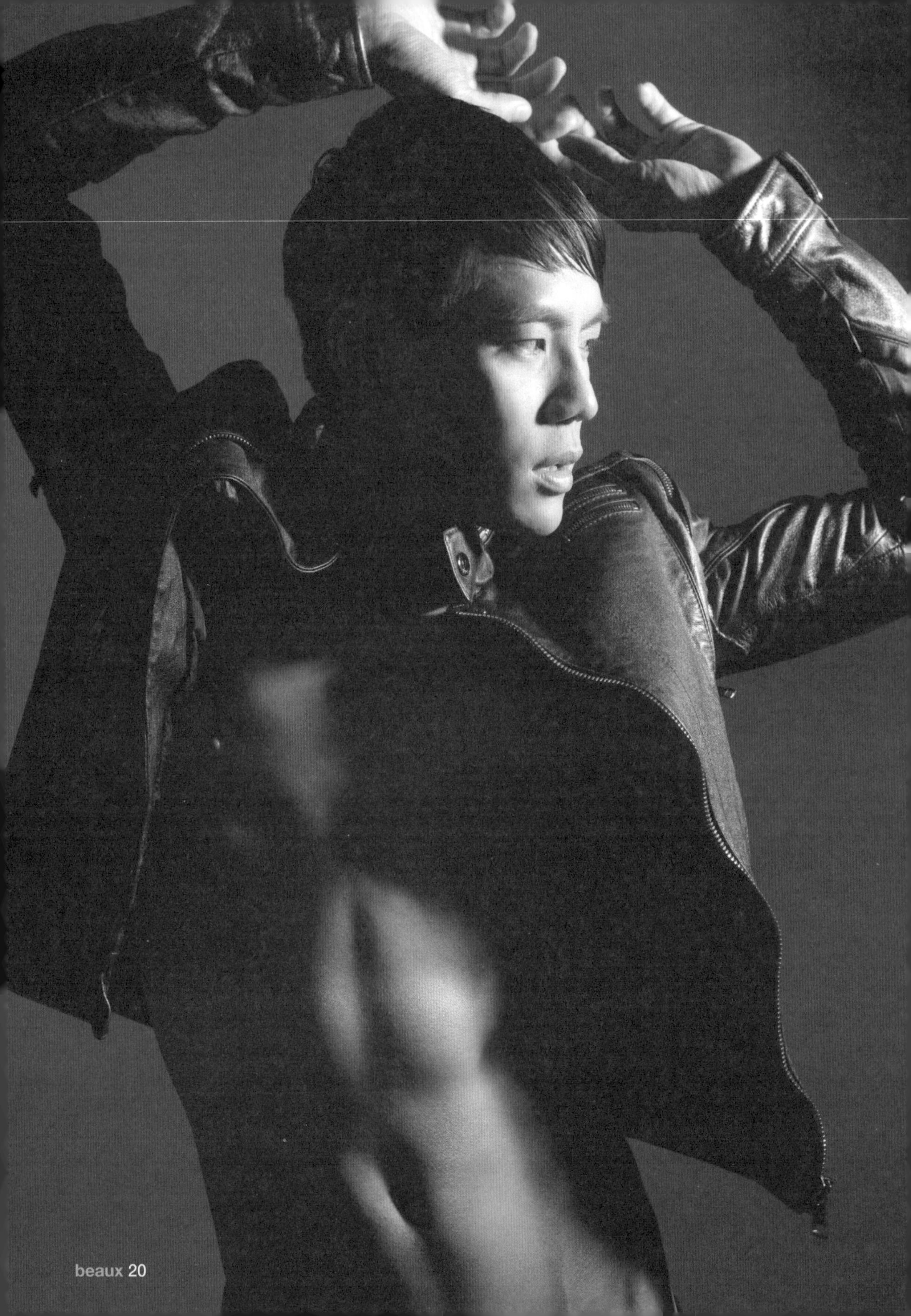

"Never underestimate a man who overestimates himself."

Franklin D. Roosevelt

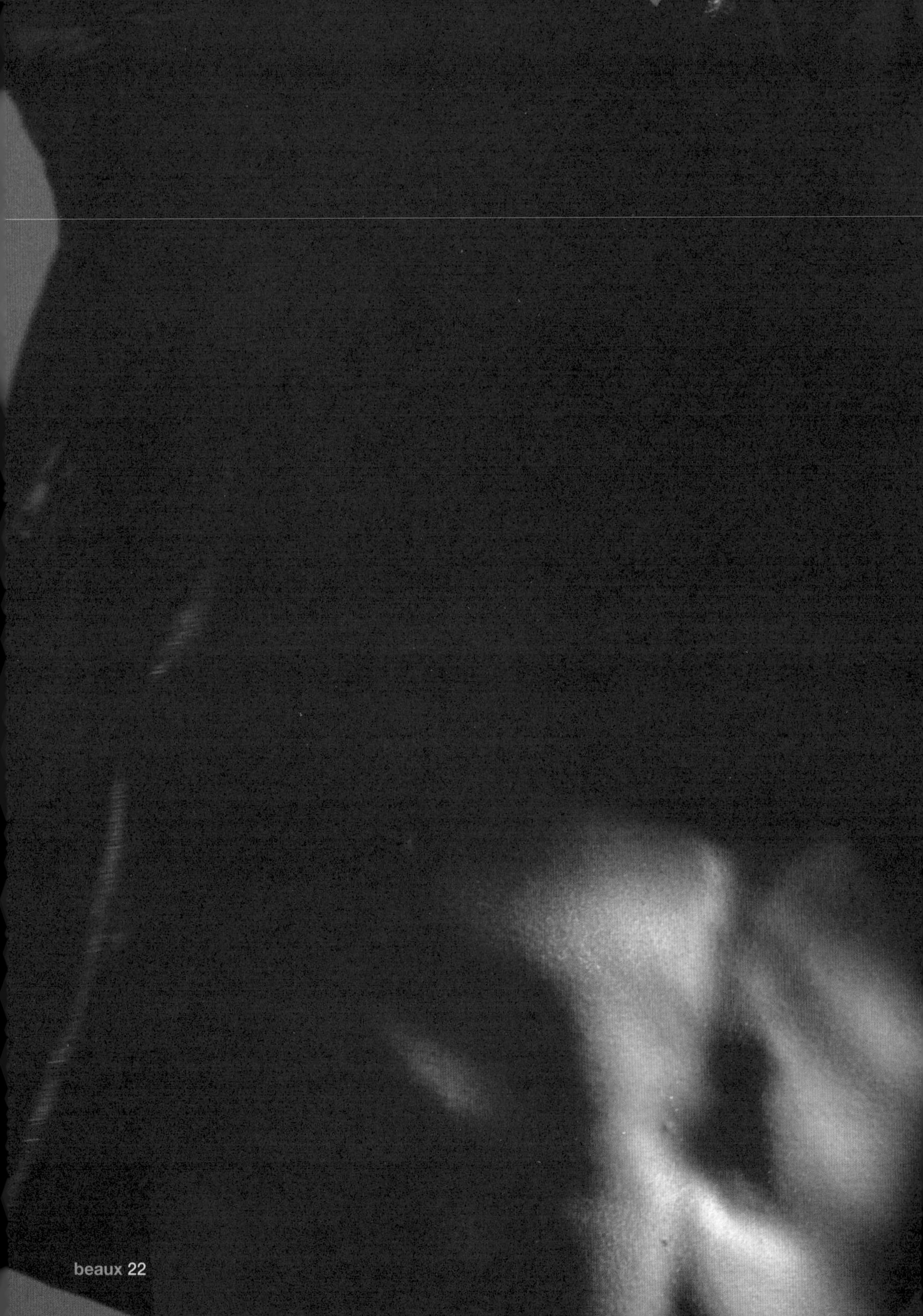

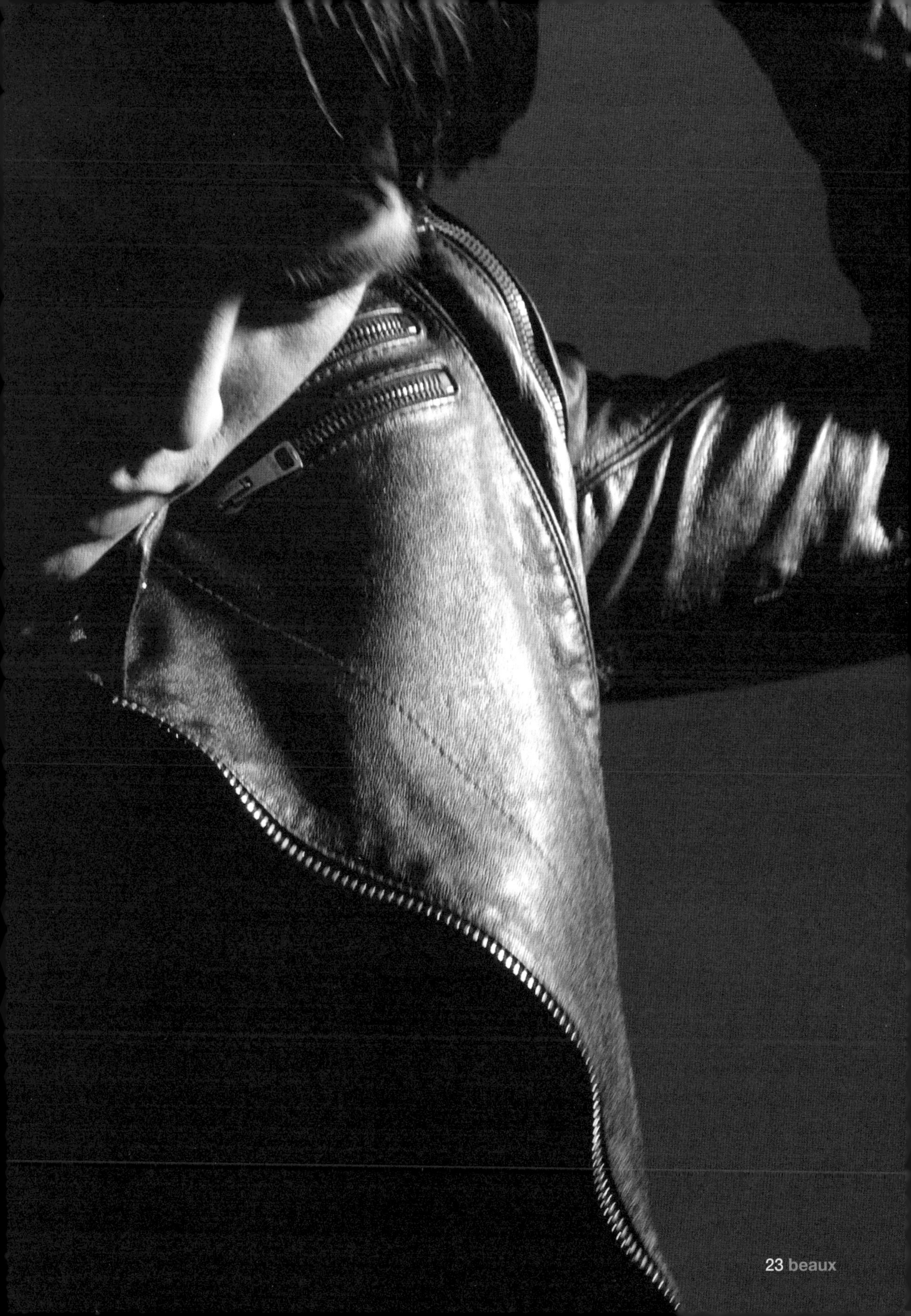

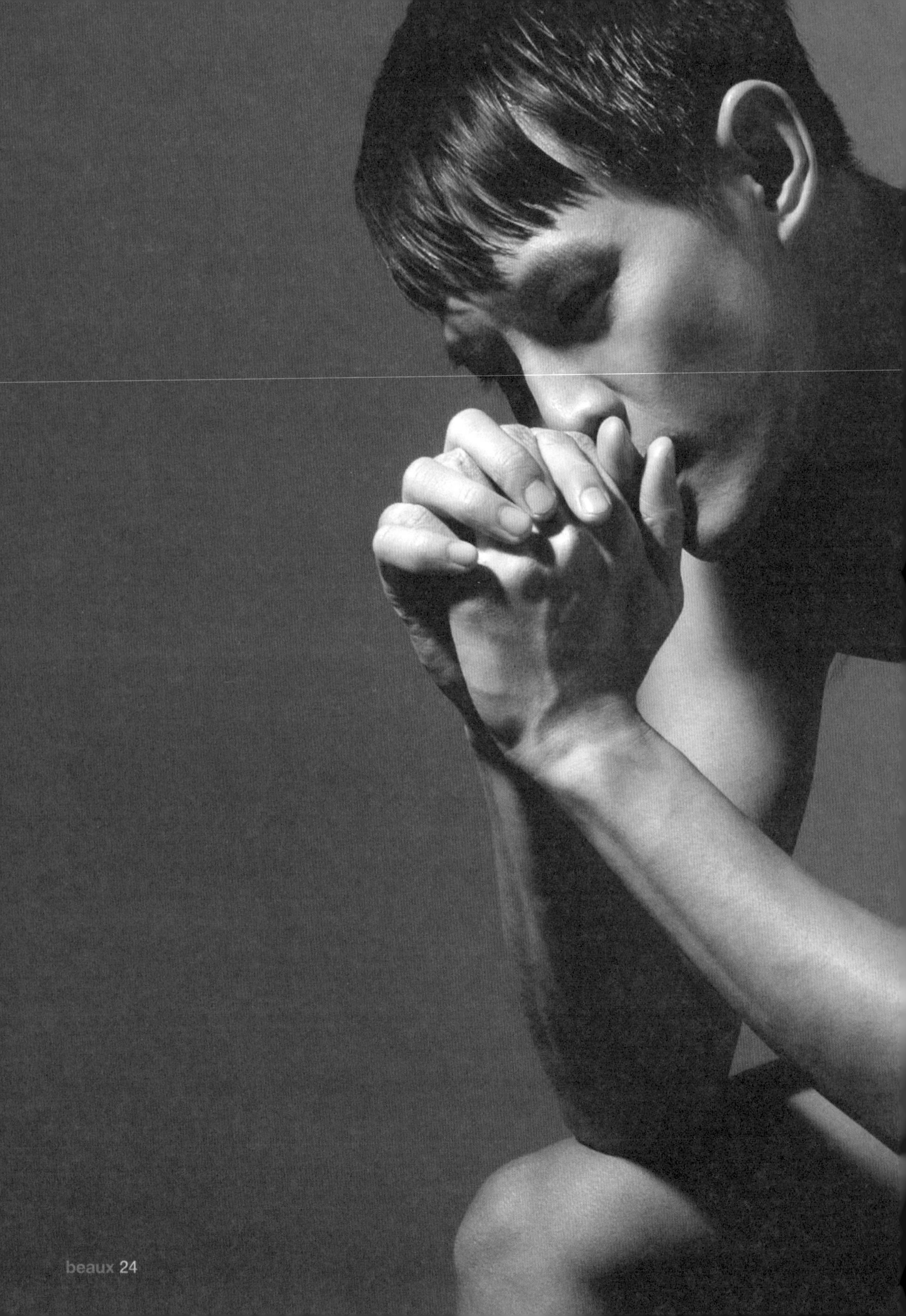

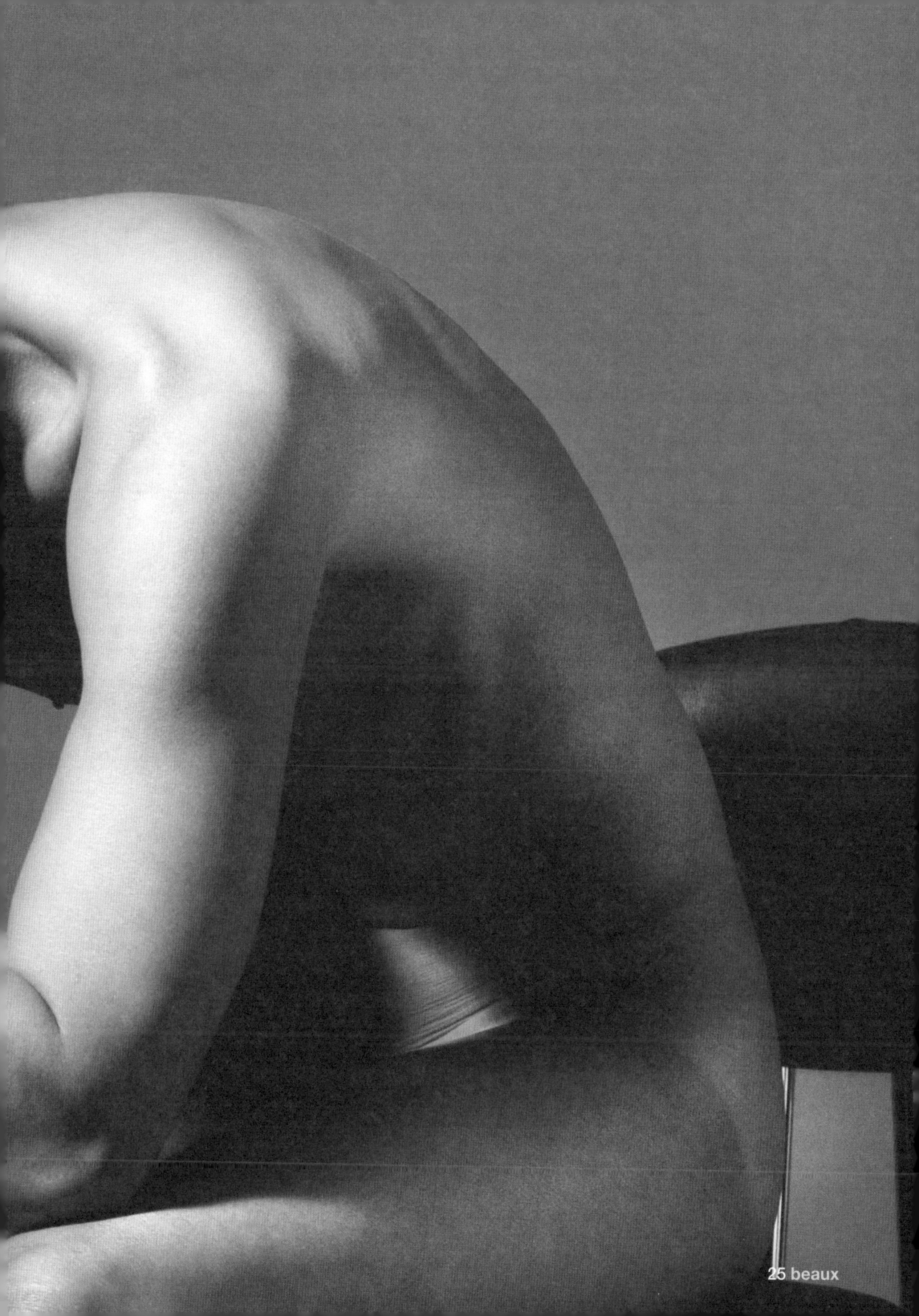

"Vanity is but the surface."

Blaise Pascal,
French Mathematician & Philosopher

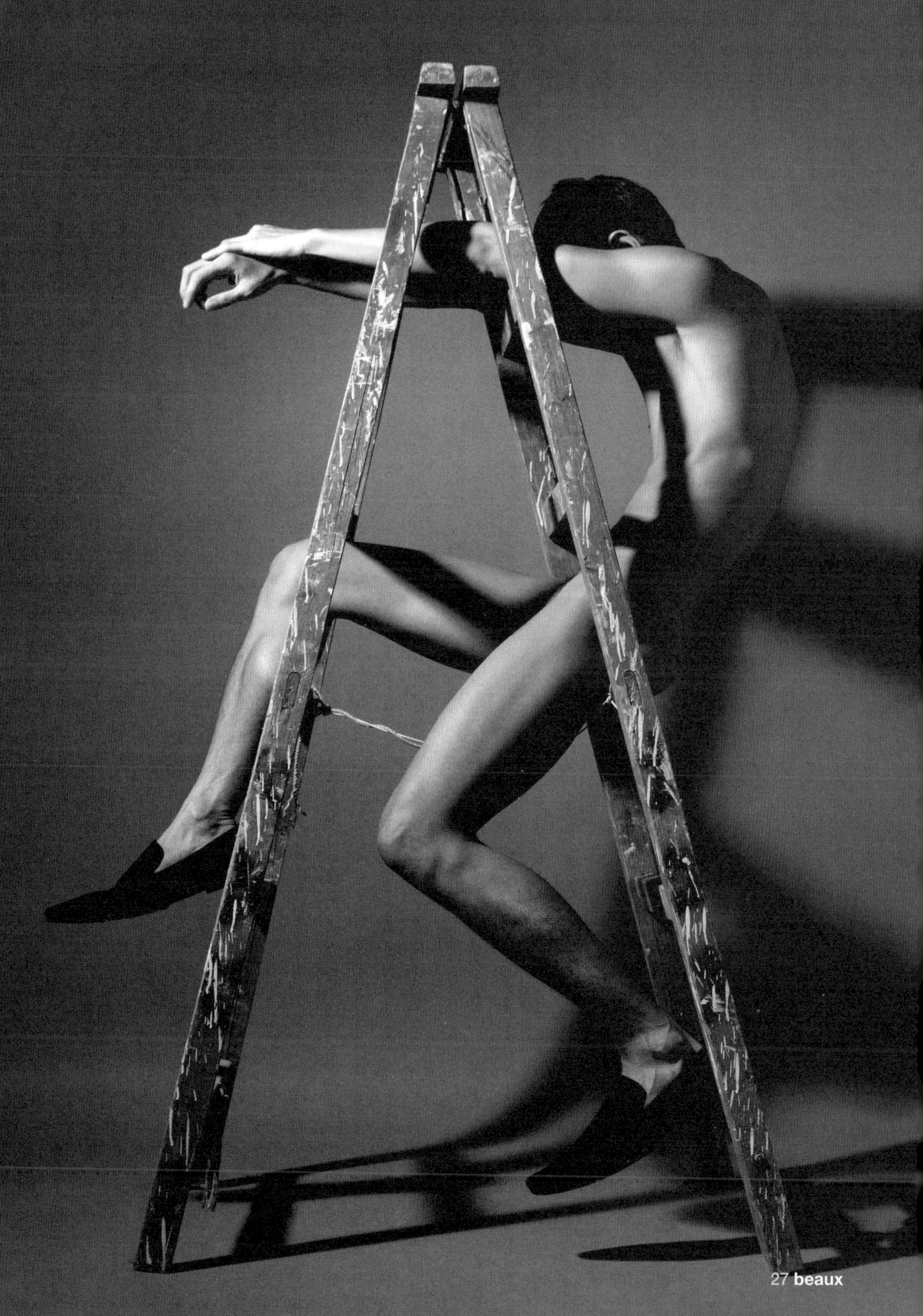

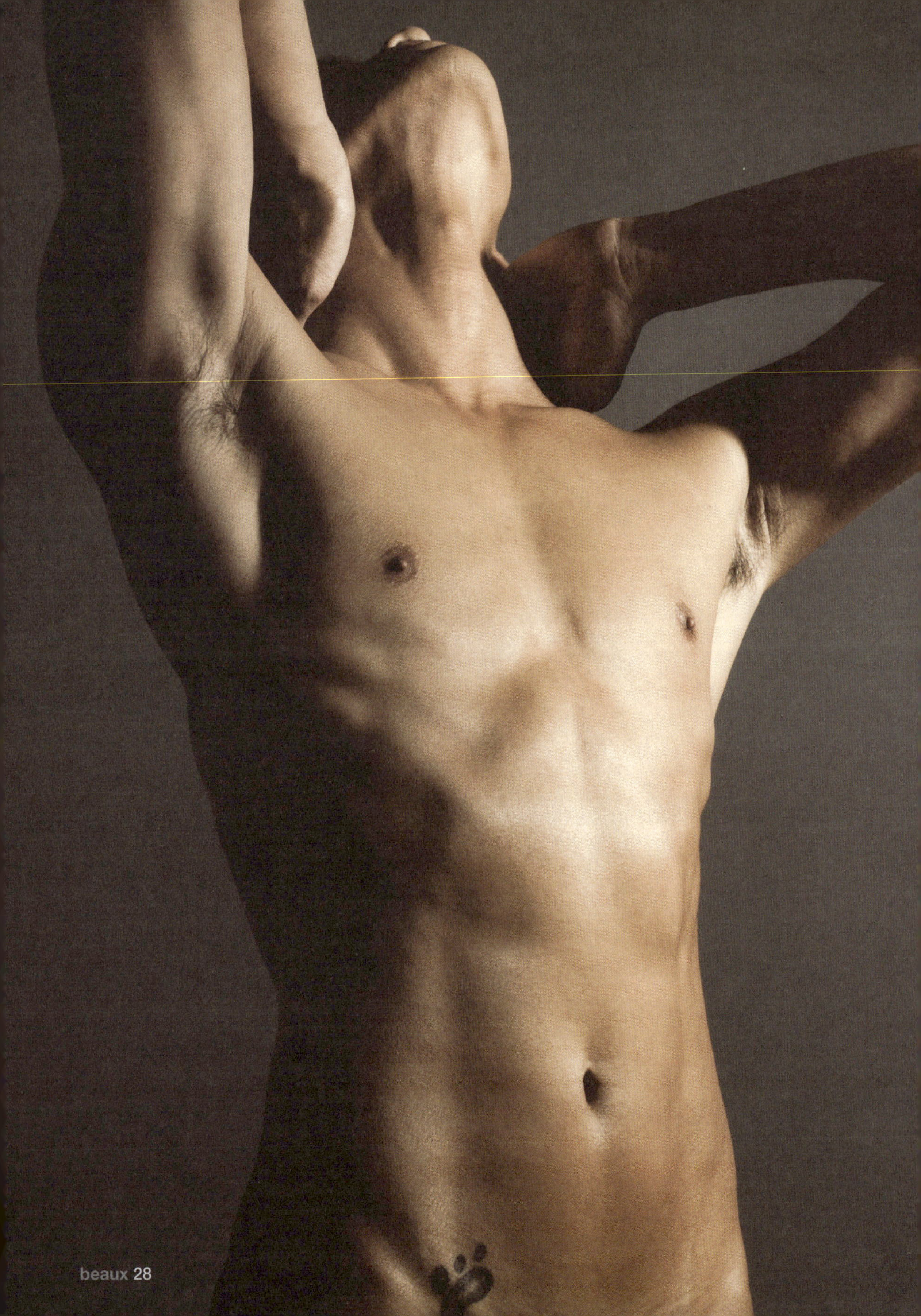

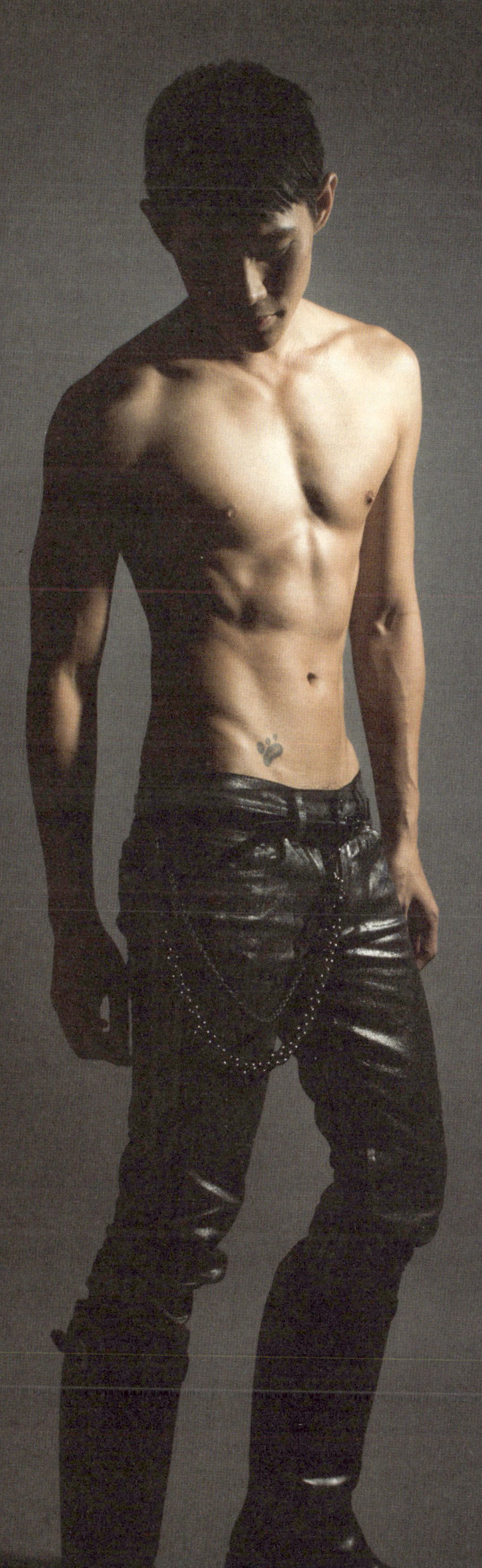

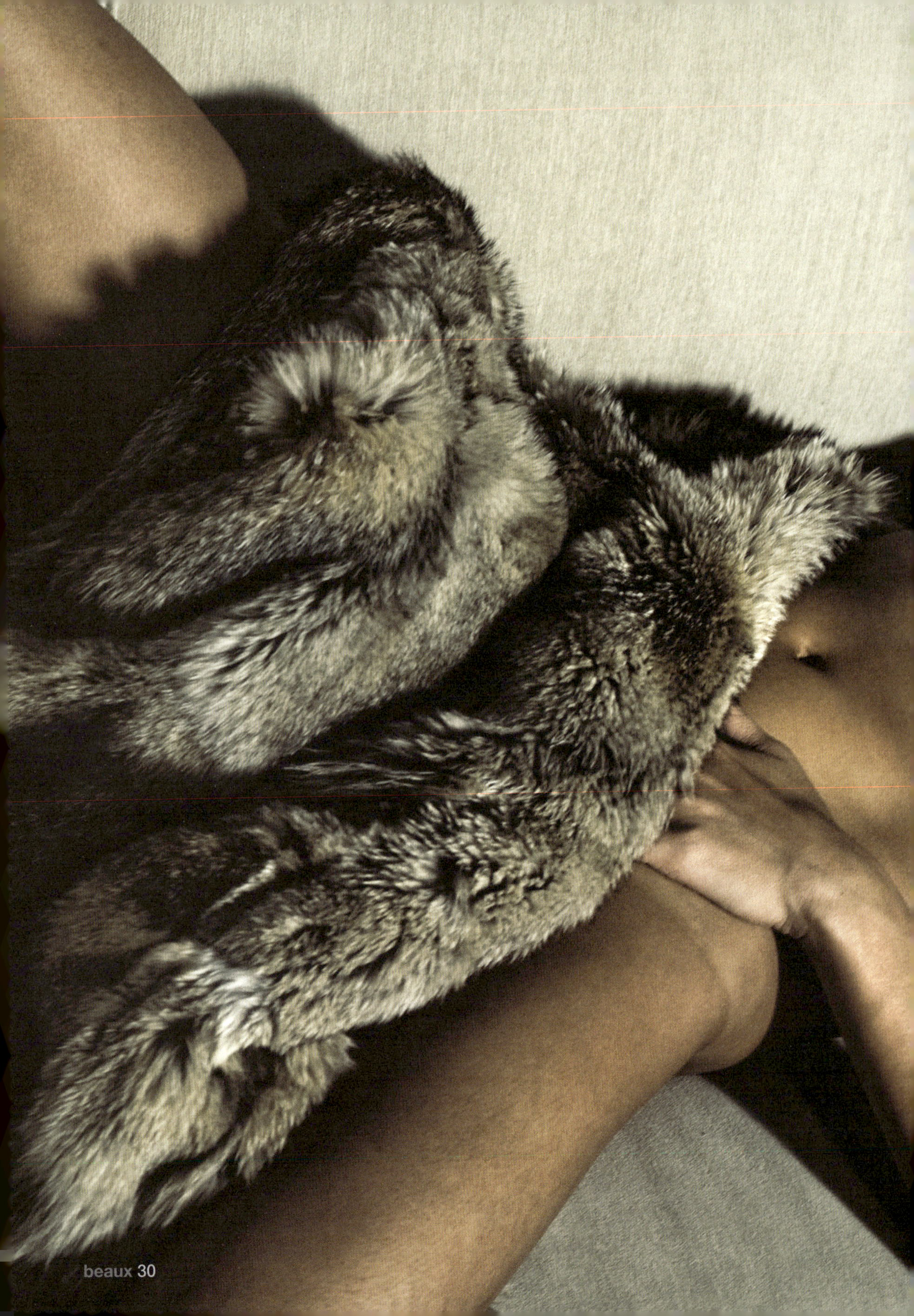

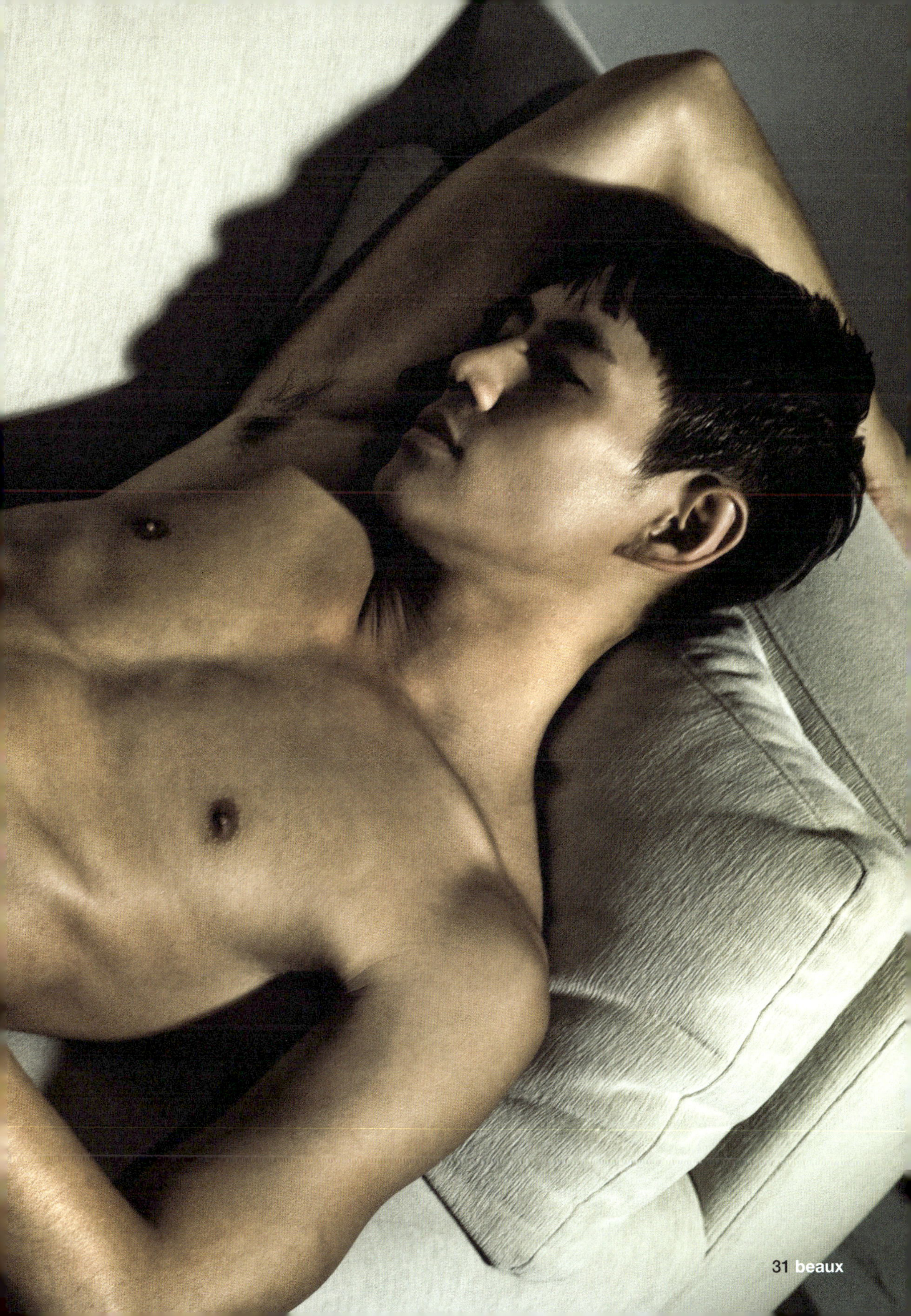

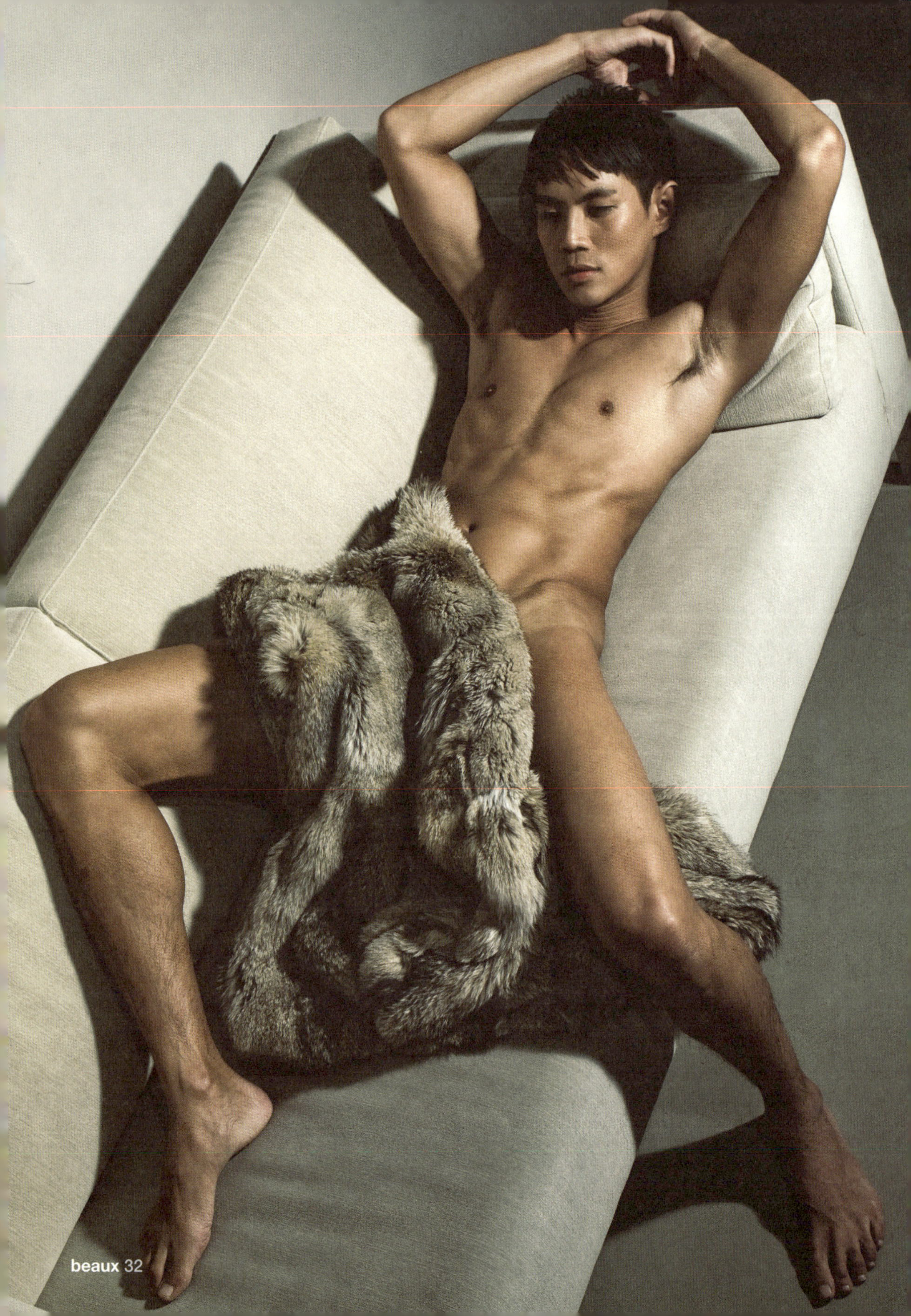

FOLIO 2

by Norm Yip

The photographs showcased in the ***folio*** *section are available for sale as signed limited edition prints. For more information, contact us at* ***enquiry@beauxmagazine.com****.*

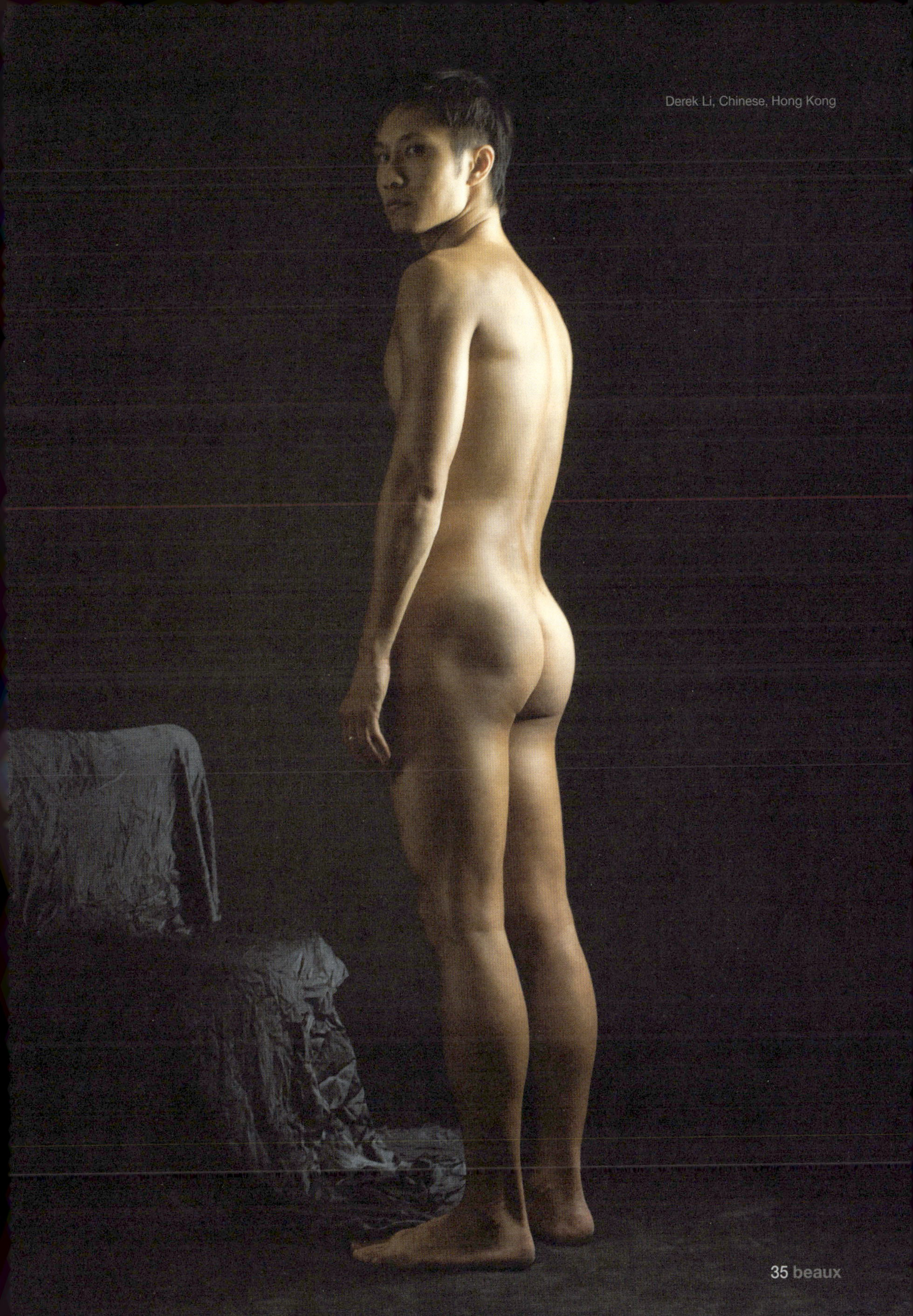

Derek Li, Chinese, Hong Kong

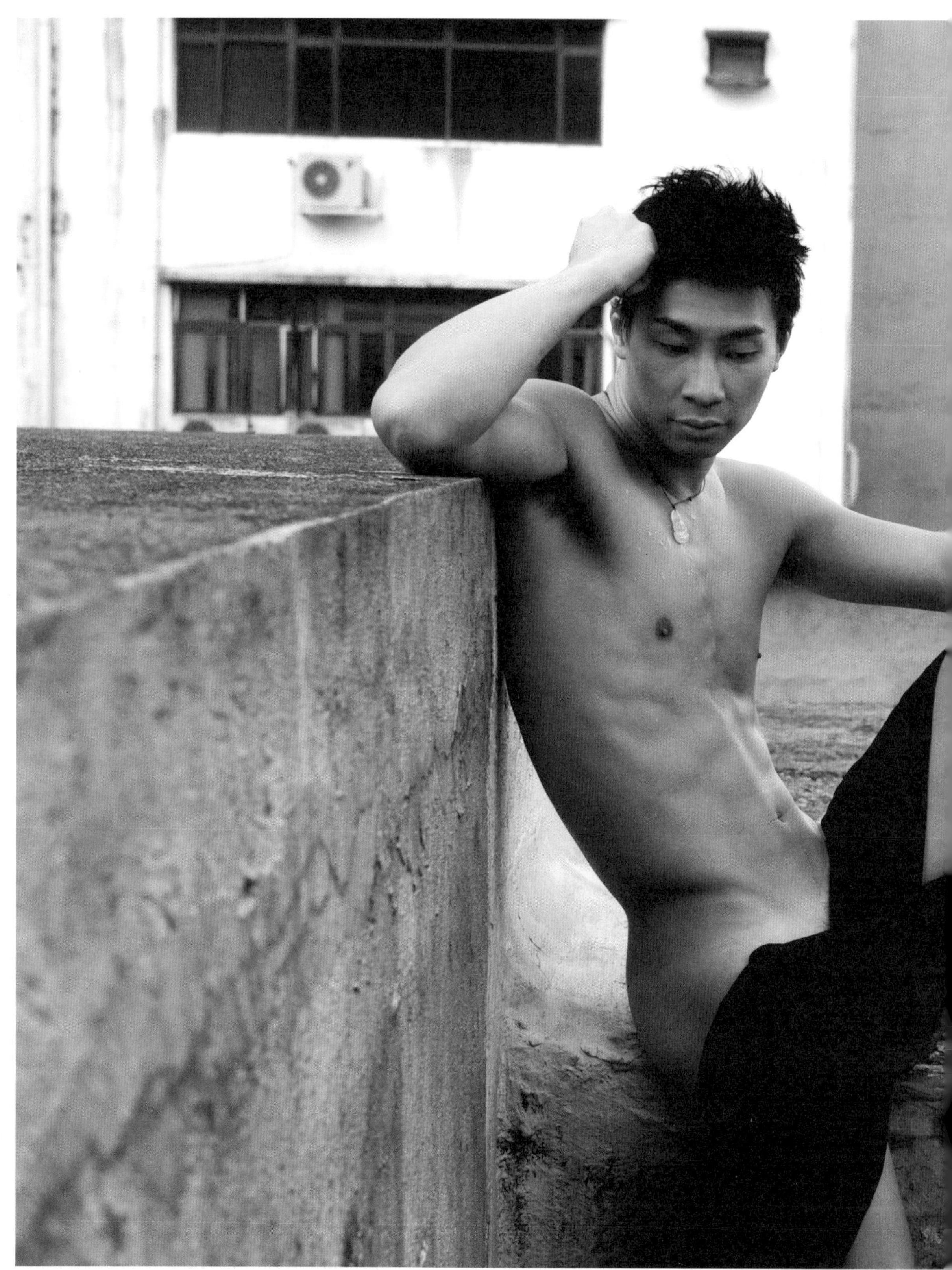

Jim Cheung, Chinese, Hong Kong

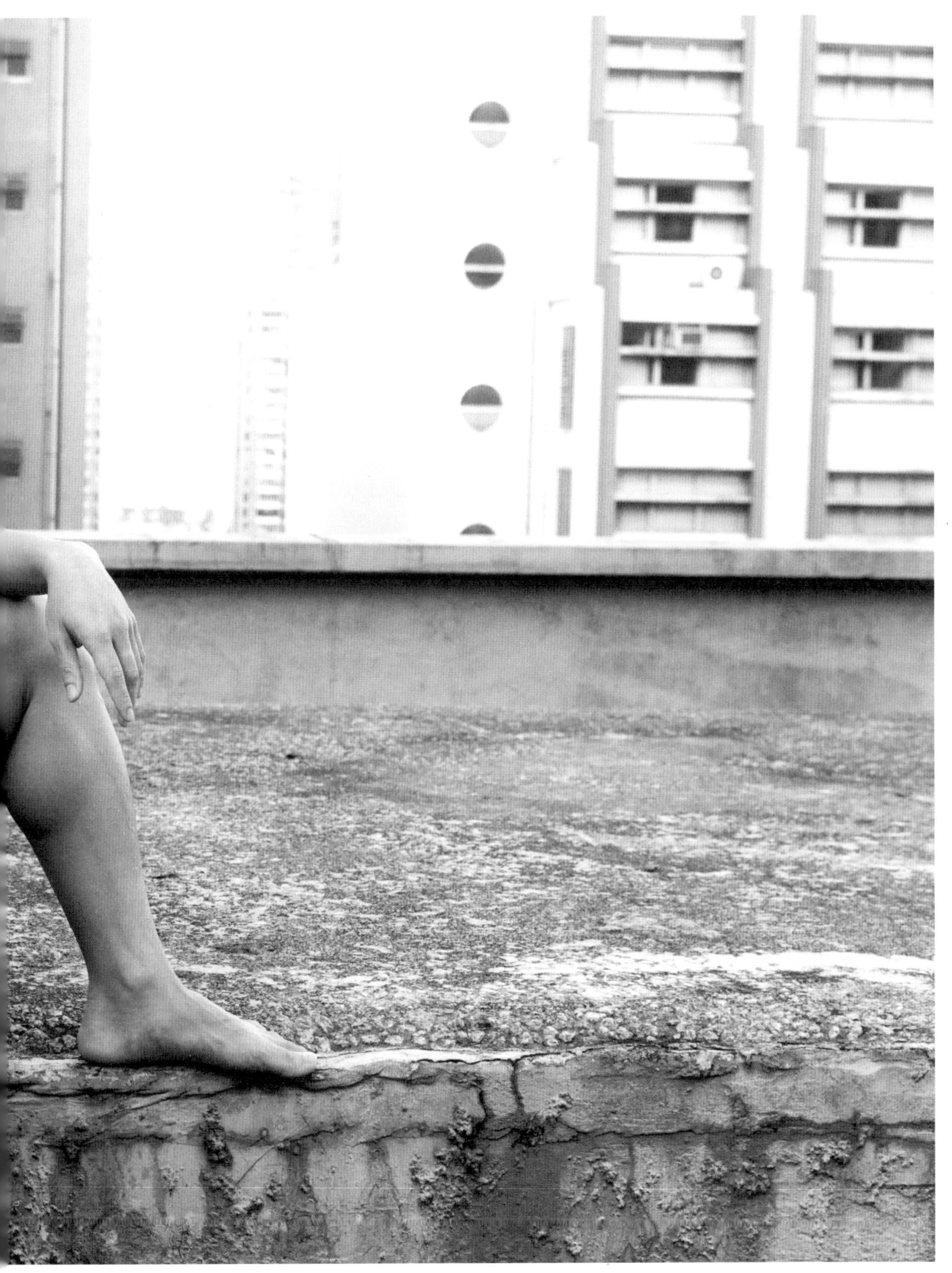

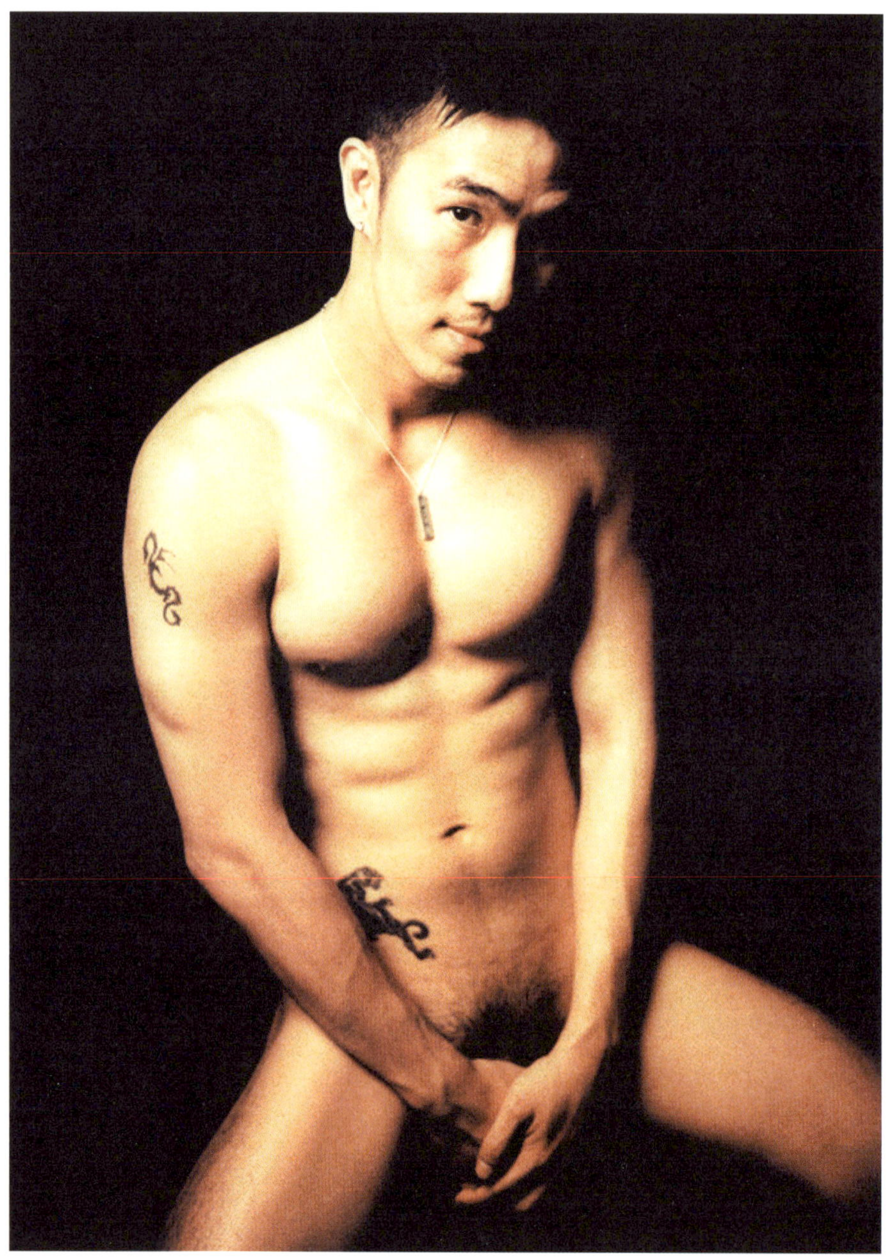

Herman Go, Chinese, United States

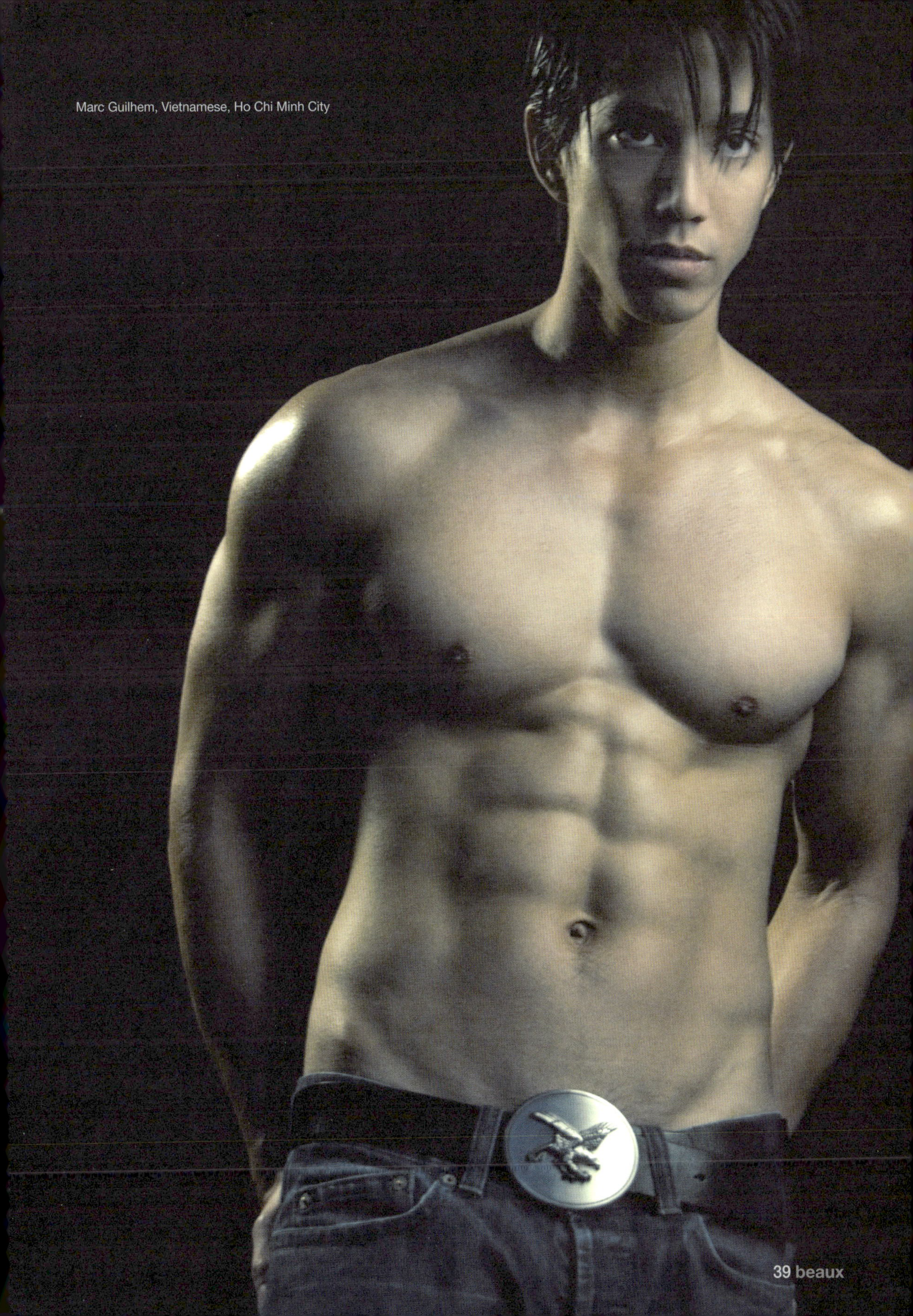
Marc Guilhem, Vietnamese, Ho Chi Minh City

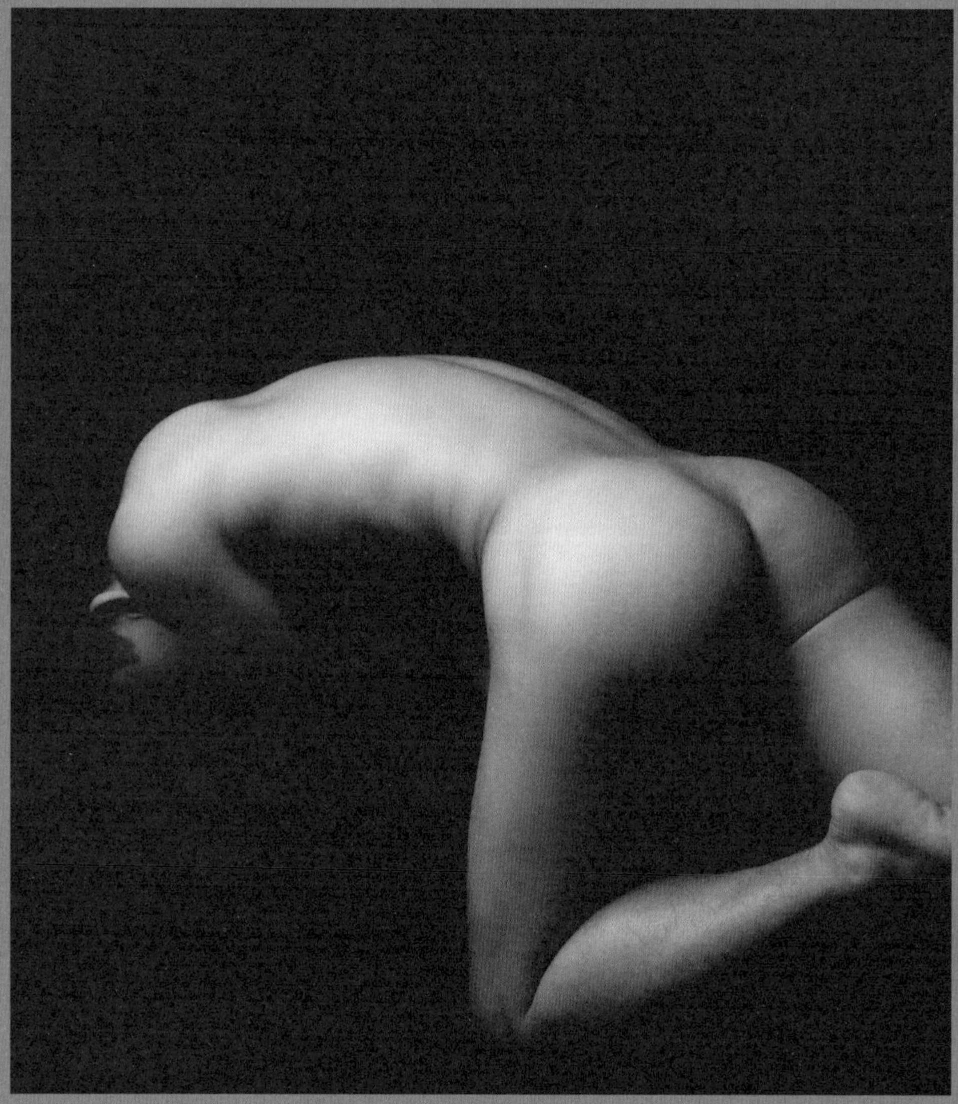

Noel Peter Tan, Filipino, Hong Kong

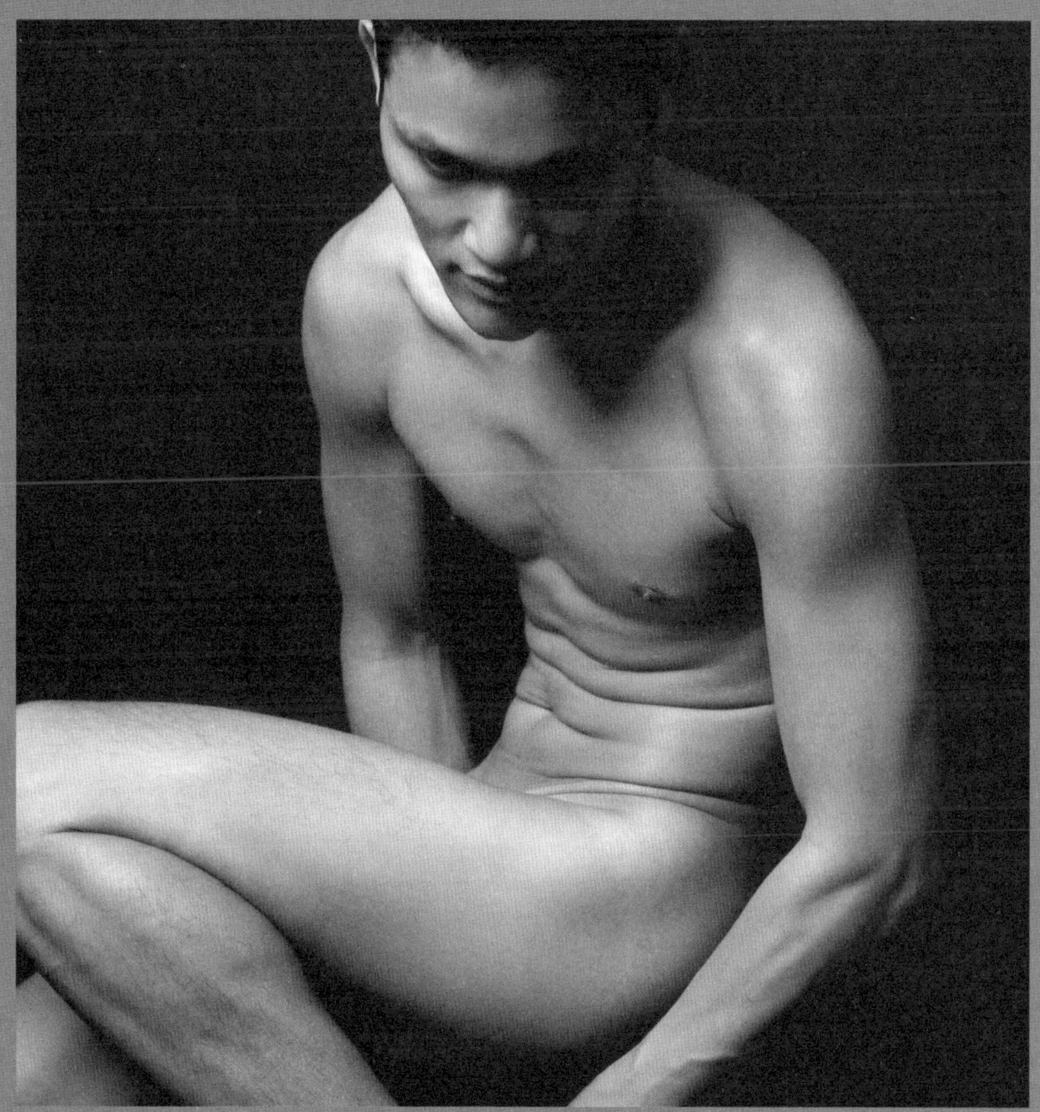

Noel Peter Tan, Filipino, Hong Kong

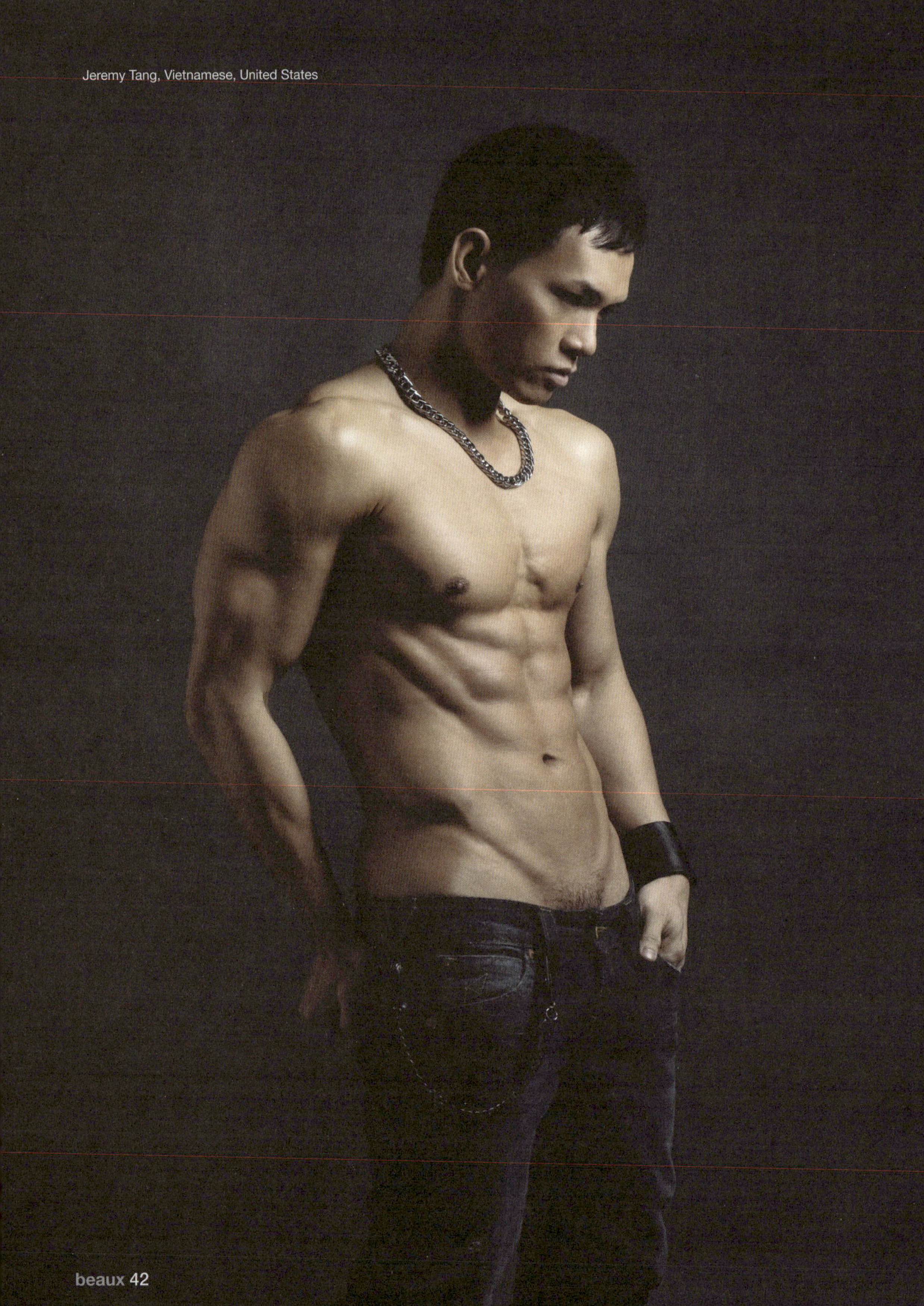

Jeremy Tang, Vietnamese, United States

Loren Tam

Interview and photography by Norm Yip

Poise. Posture. Polish.

I was honoured to photograph this Hong Kong native at my Chai Wan studio where we spent a few hours exploring his skills in front of the camera – stripping his inhibitions away with his clothes, piece by piece. Exuding an enigmatic blend of masculinity and boyish charm, Loren Tam discusses his love for figure skating and shares his favourite workout routine. In-between takes, I got to know him a little better as we chatted about his profession, his travel experience and even about hanging out with his friends.

Loren, tell us something about yourself and your background.

I was born and raised in Hong Kong. I finished university, majoring in English and translation. Now, I work in public relations. I also have a younger sister.

What are some of your hobbies and general activities? Favorite movies? Travel?

I like to travel a lot. It's a great way to leave the familiar world and to absorb something new. I absolutely enjoy meeting different people and experiencing unfamiliar cultures, different languages and exotic food!

But most of the time, I enjoy chilling out with my good friends, having a drink, trying out new restaurants, or watching a movie. I enjoy watching performing arts, especially dances. Some friends of mine are big fans of the film and arts festivals in Hong Kong.

In the past, I also used to sketch and paint a lot. But I stopped after school. Recently, I've been thinking of taking it up again. In terms of sports, I play tennis and I have been practicing figure skating on and off for 10 years now.

What's your perception of men from Hong Kong? Can you see any distinguishable differences, let's say, in looks between Hong Kongnese men and Singaporean men or those from Thailand, Korea or Japan?

I don't want to over-generalize Asian men because they are as diverse as any other guys in other parts of the world. That being said, I find Hong Kongnese men in particular to be more traditional in terms of looks and values but more adventurous than other Asian men in other respects.

Photographing you was an enjoyable experience for me. How was it? Was it your first time in front of a professional photographer?

Yes. It was my first time and it was enjoyable too. I was a little bit nervous in the beginning, but I got more comfortable towards the end. Thanks Norm ;)

You allowed me to photograph you nude. Tell me what it was like.

It was very interesting. Aside from my nervousness, I was surprised that I did much better than I had thought. As the shoot went on, I felt that there was no difference in whether I had my clothes on or off! The only weird thing was that I felt my poses were becoming too repetitive. I was such a big bore!

Some of your photographs were very sensual and some even erotic. What are your thoughts when the body becomes a piece of art? Has your experience made you connect with the images that you were portraying?

Knowing that your body can be represented as a piece of art is great. I studied art in school and I was mesmerized by the beauty of the human body as

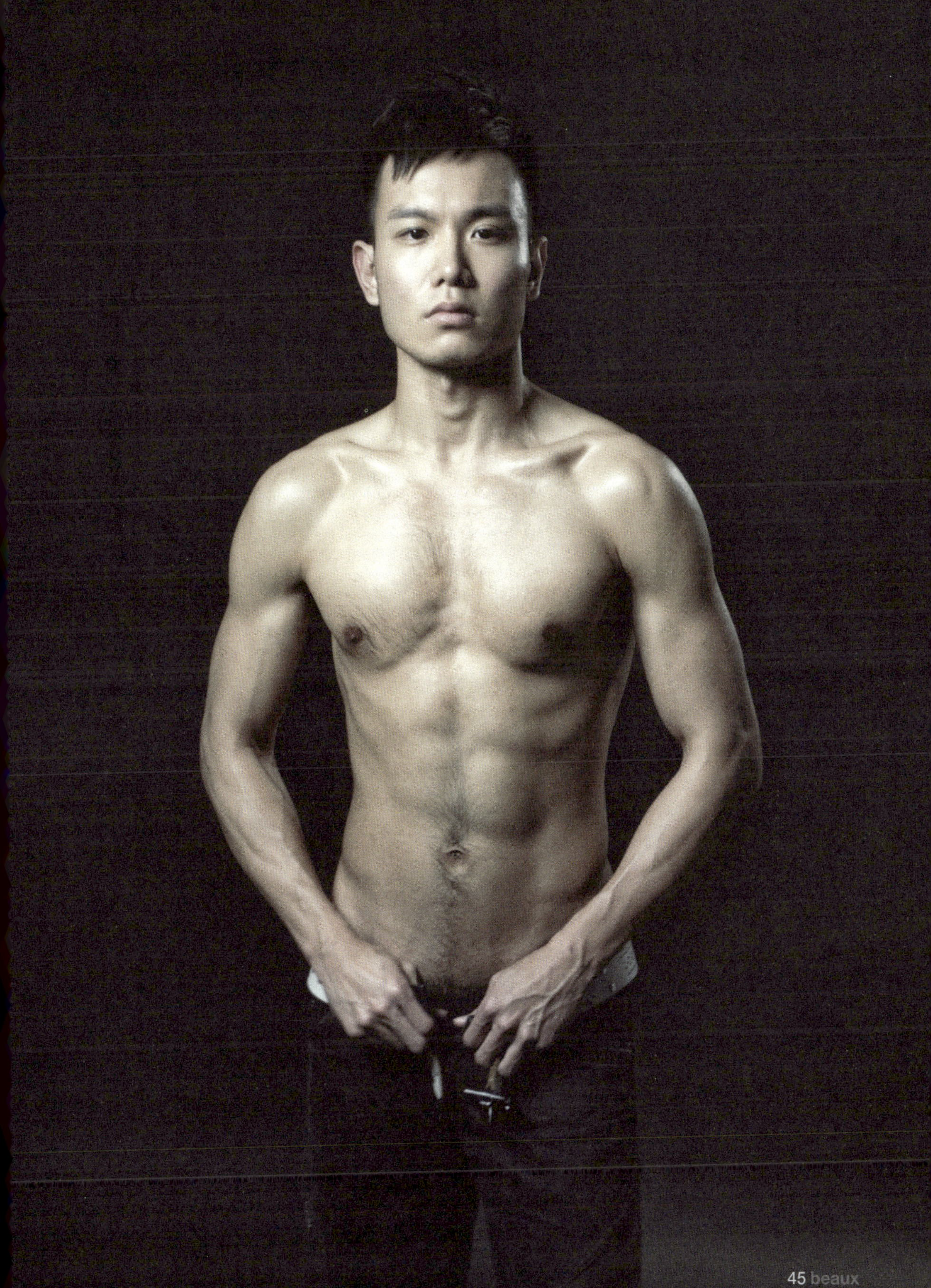

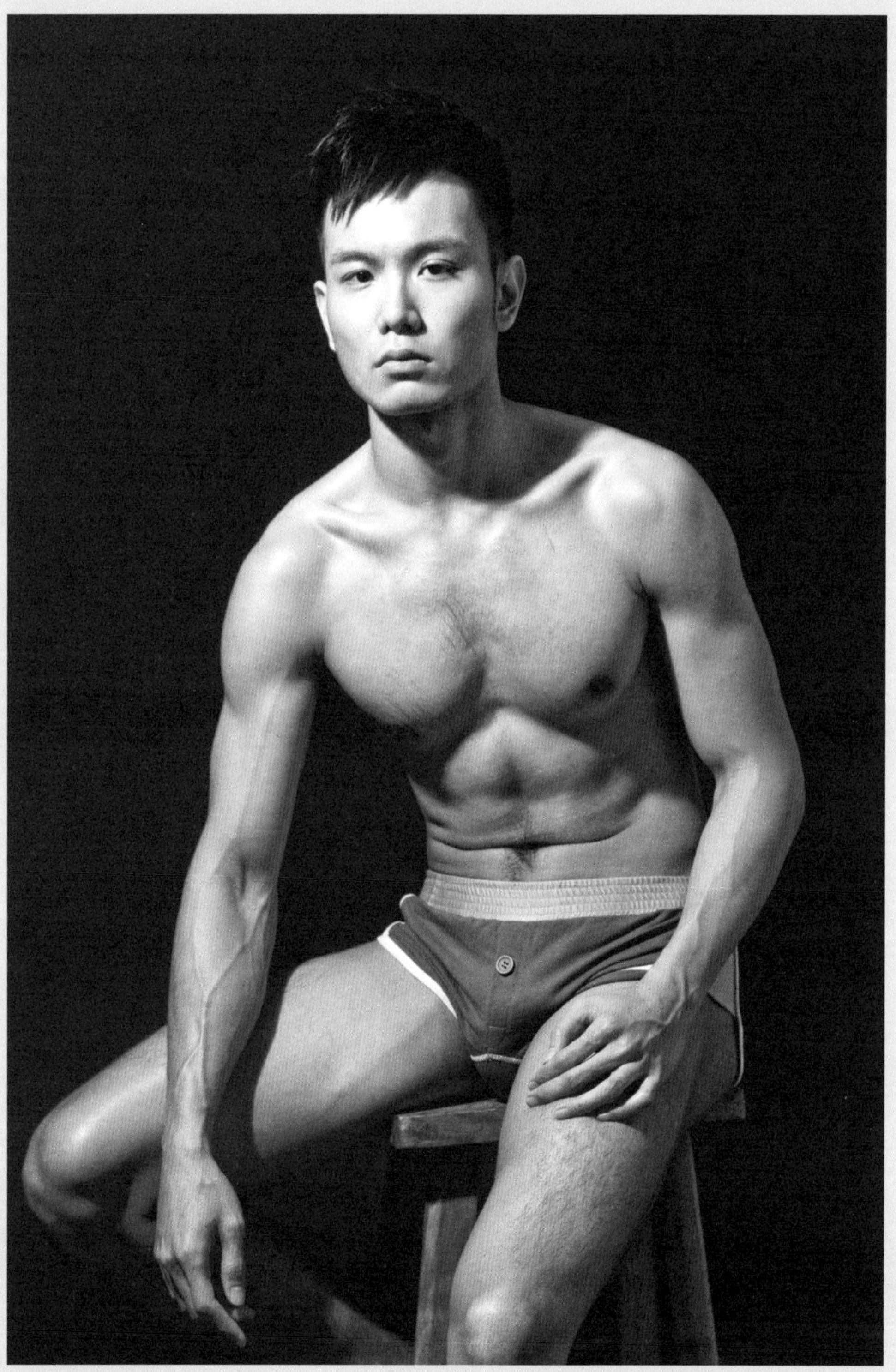

portrayed in sculptures and in paintings. In some of my photographs, I felt a deep connection with them. It was a matter of how much I can express myself during this shoot. It wasn't easy but then again, I'm not a professional model.

Speaking of the body and physique, how do you feel about your own body? Is there too much emphasis on appearance rather than education and knowledge these days?

I feel great about my body. I work hard to make it look good which in turn makes me feel great. Still, my muscles are not as developed compared with some other guys out there. I only work out three times a week. My body, my personality, and the embodiment of my spirit are what my family and friends appreciate. I am a happy man as long as they like who I am.

A friend asked me to ask you the following question: If given the choice, would you prefer to have a good-looking face with an average body or an average face with a good-looking body?

Can't I have both? Well, perhaps I will go for a better looking face. You don't have many chances to show off your naked body in front of the camera, right? But you use your face to greet people with and having the right 'look' can open the right doors for you. Of course, there are other things that will take you a long way; a great personality, wisdom, wealth… take your pick.

What is your workout routine? And how did you get those muscular legs? They are very impressive!

I work out 2 to 3 times a week. Now I do weight training on my upper-body and arms. I run on the treadmill for 35 minutes once a week. As I haven't been training properly, I tend to do more workstation workouts than free weight ones; I don't want to hurt myself.

For my legs, they used to be even more muscular! My thighs were so big that I couldn't find a pair of jeans that fit. I stopped practicing figure skating after university and my thighs got slightly slimmer. Thank goodness! I've picked up skating again for almost a year now. This sport has certainly trained my legs again.

Do you have any specific goals or aspirations for your future? Any philosophy on how you live your life?

Just stay happy. It sounds easy but it requires a lot of discipline. Yes, that's how I see it.

shootout

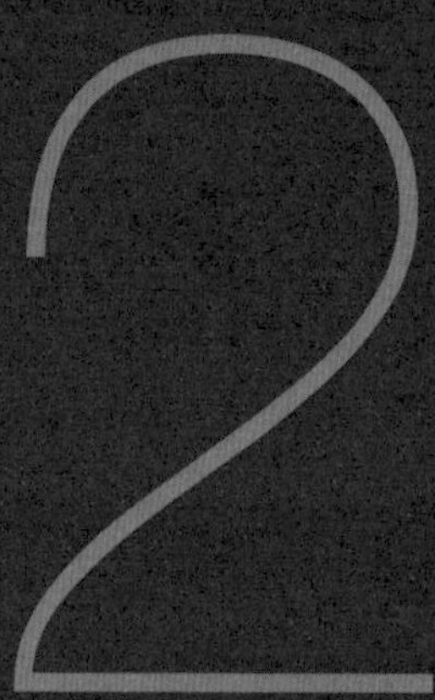

Photographer Norm Yip
Model Patrick Lui, Chinese, Hong Kong
Location Studio 8

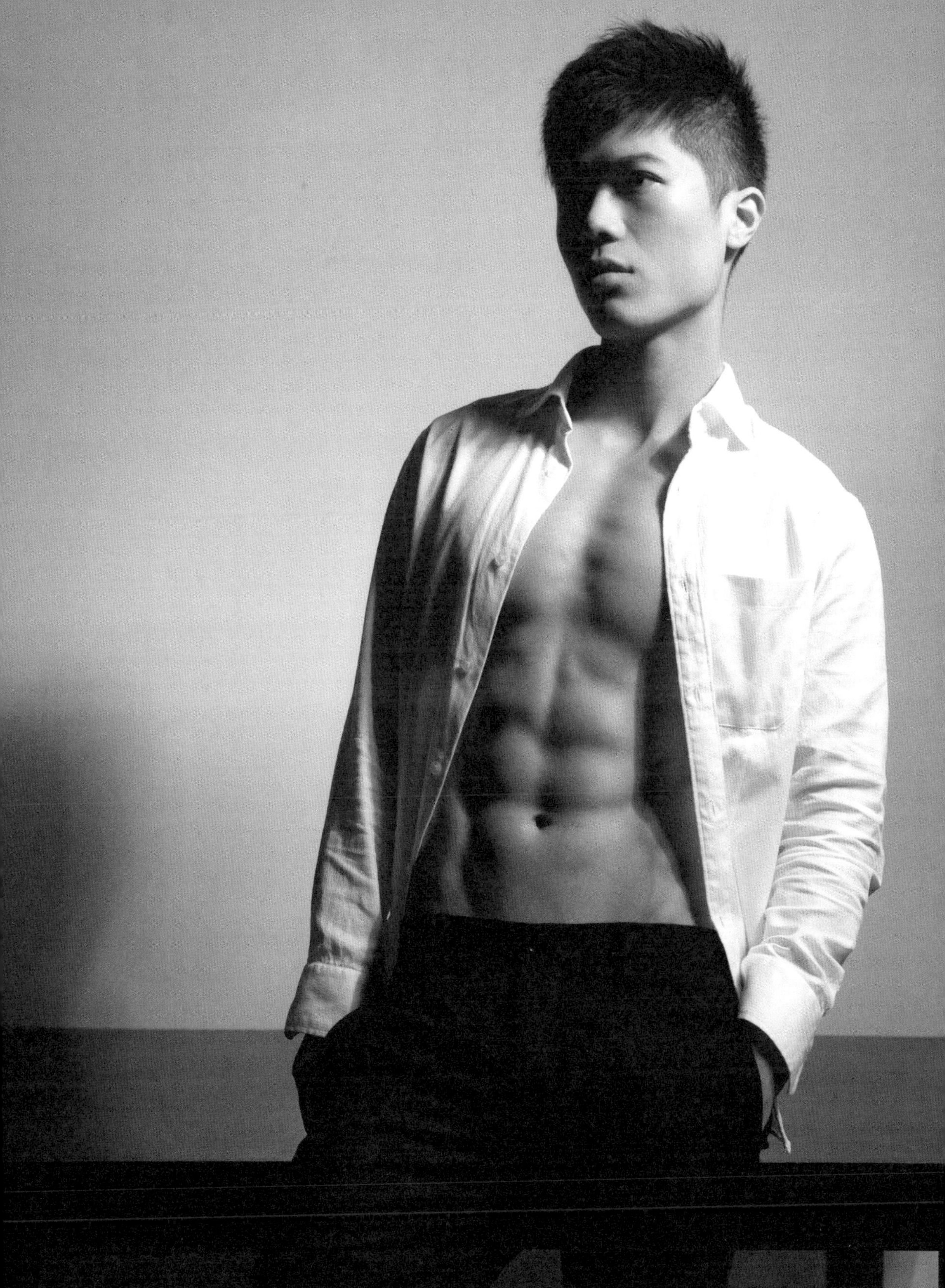

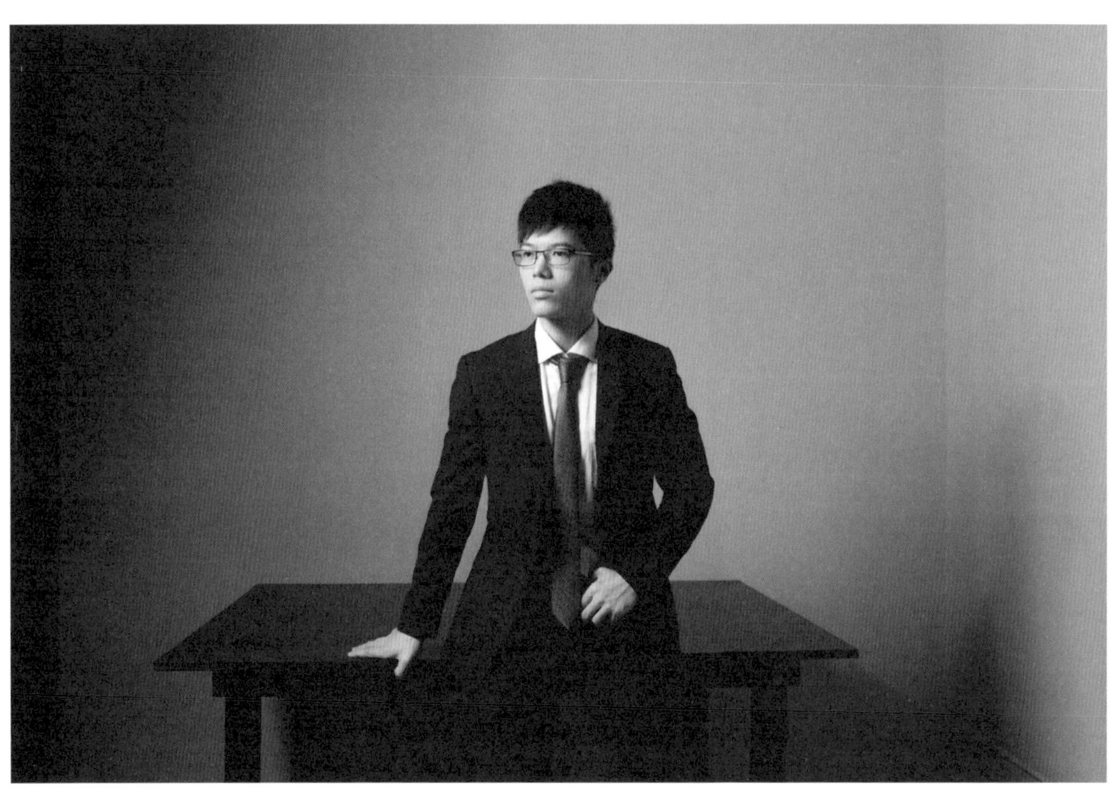

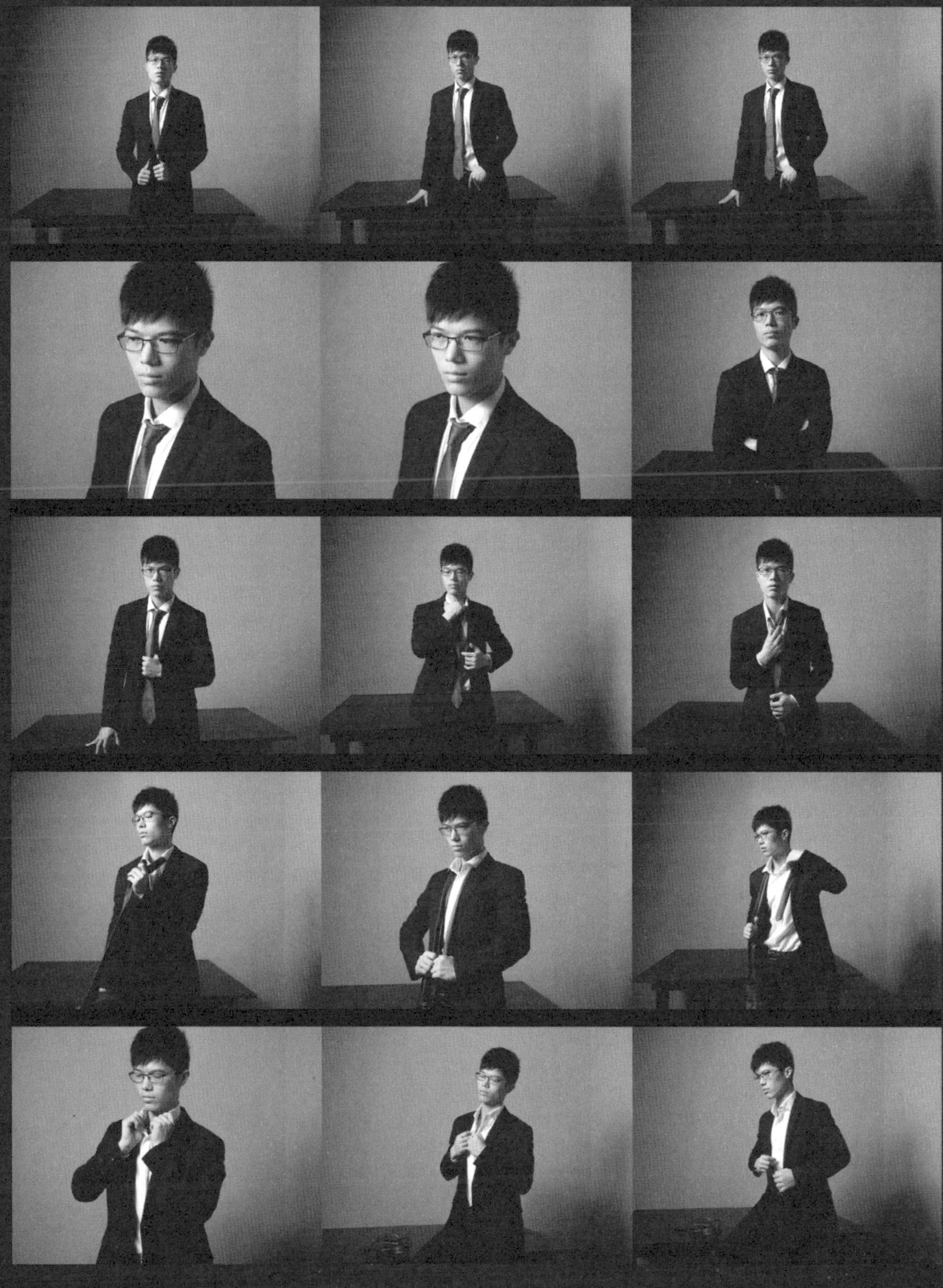

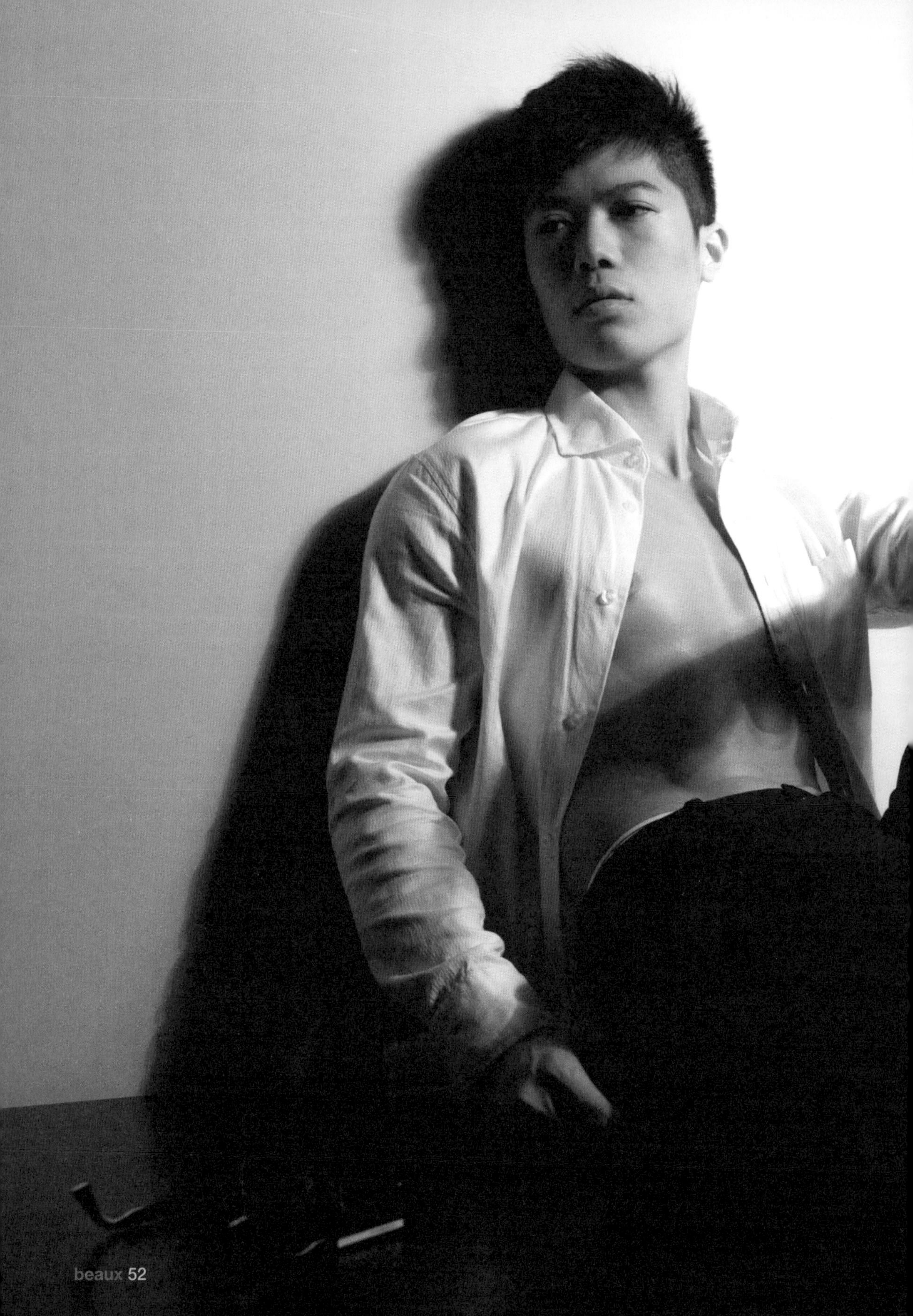

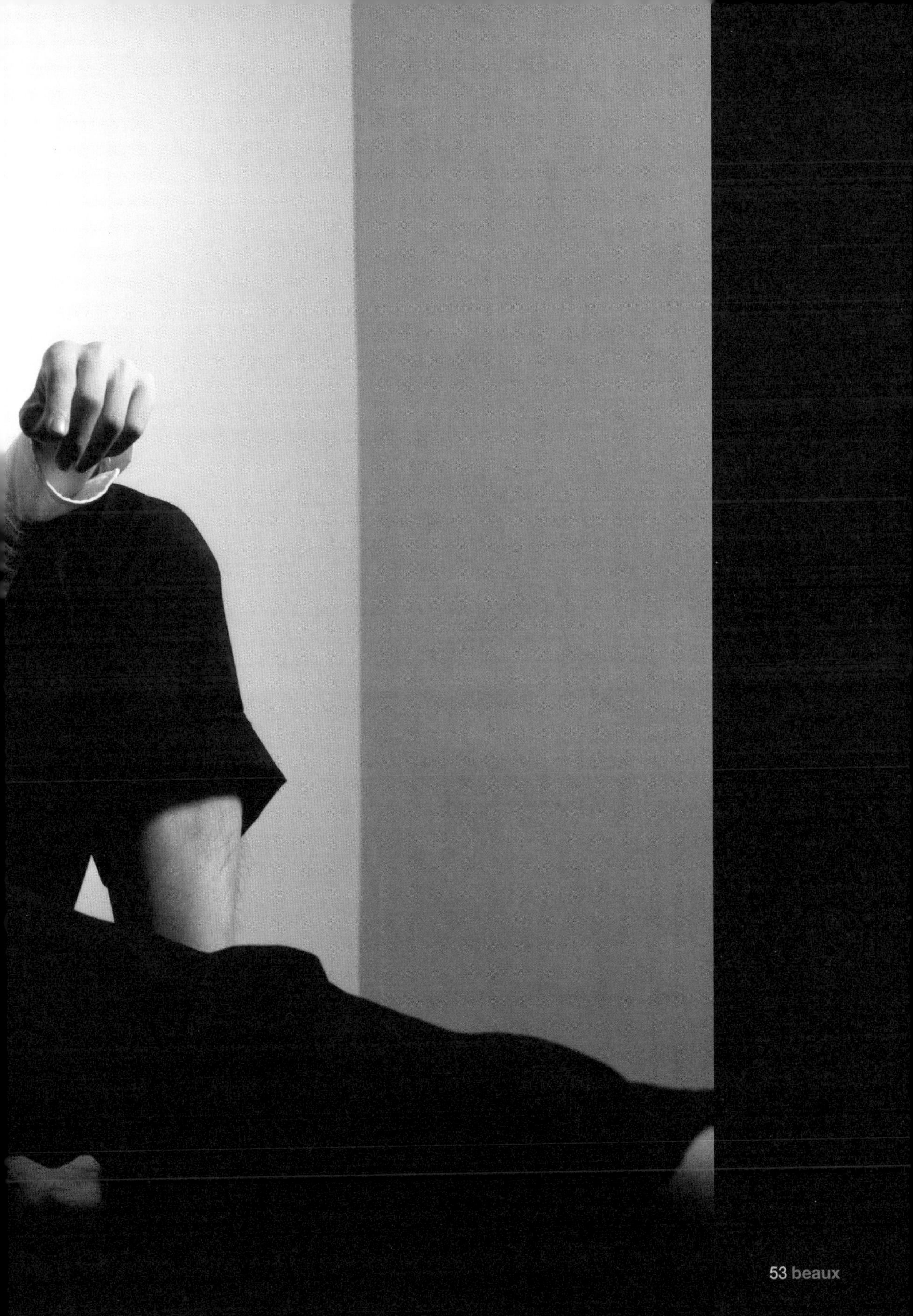

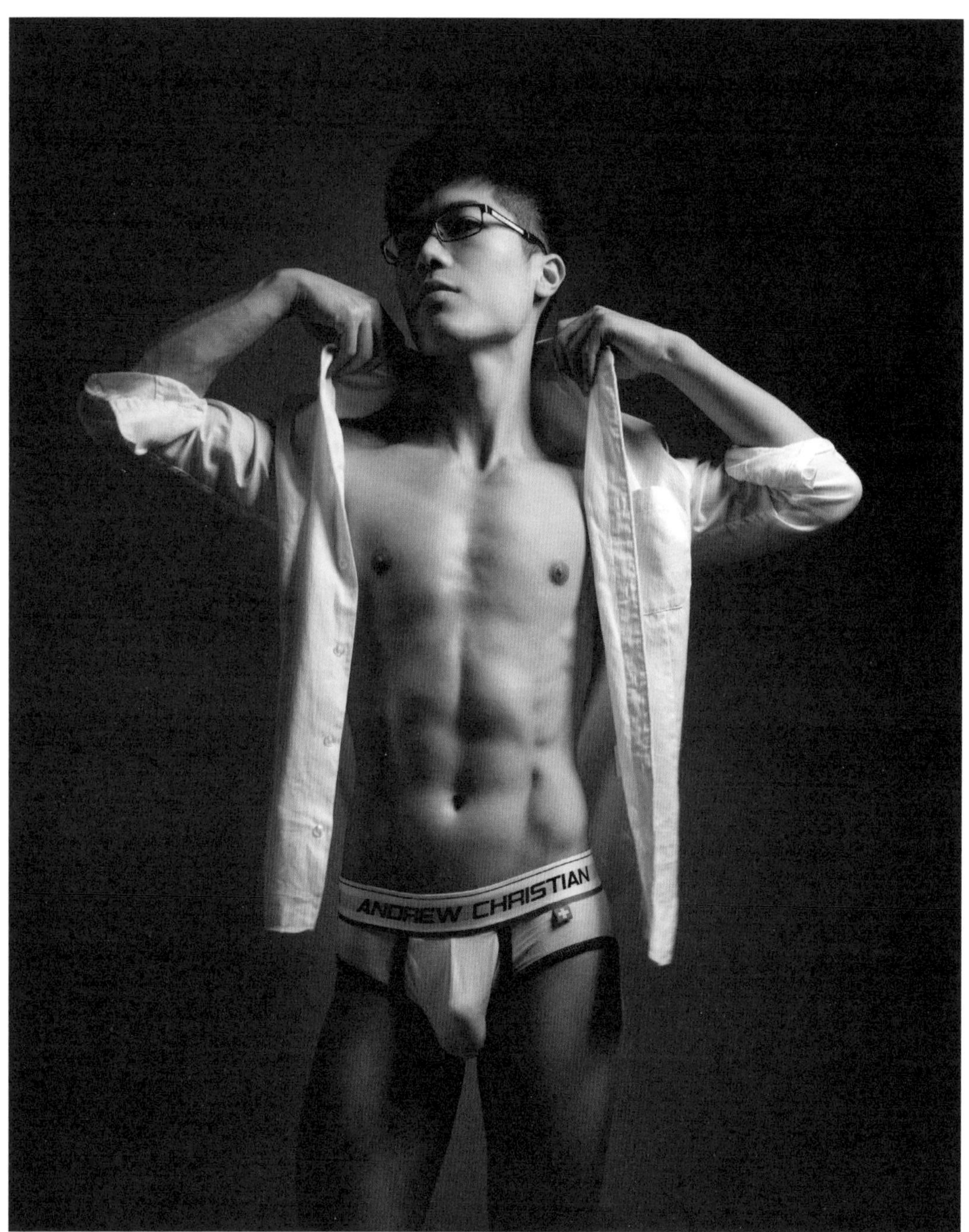
ANDREW CHRISTIAN

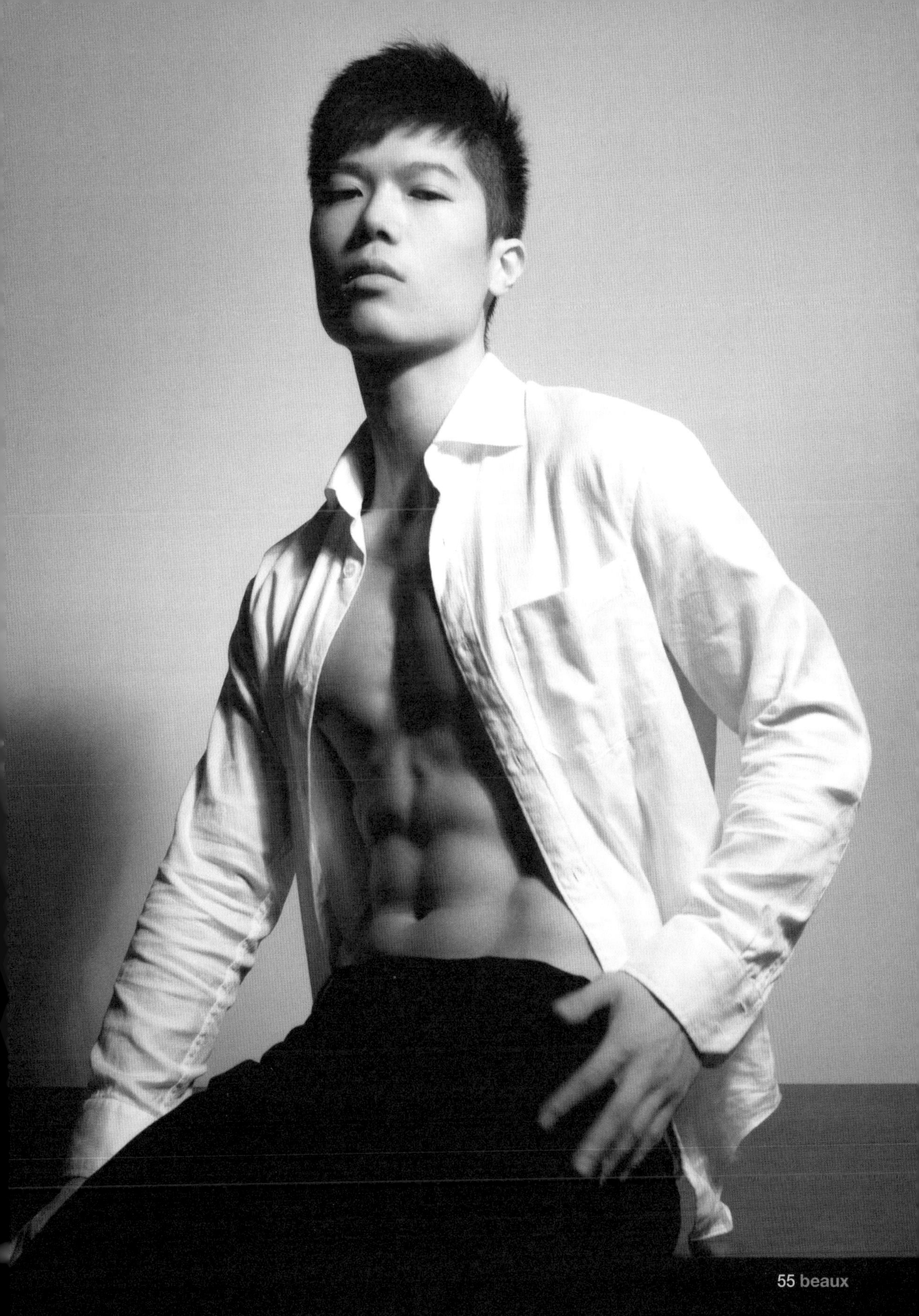

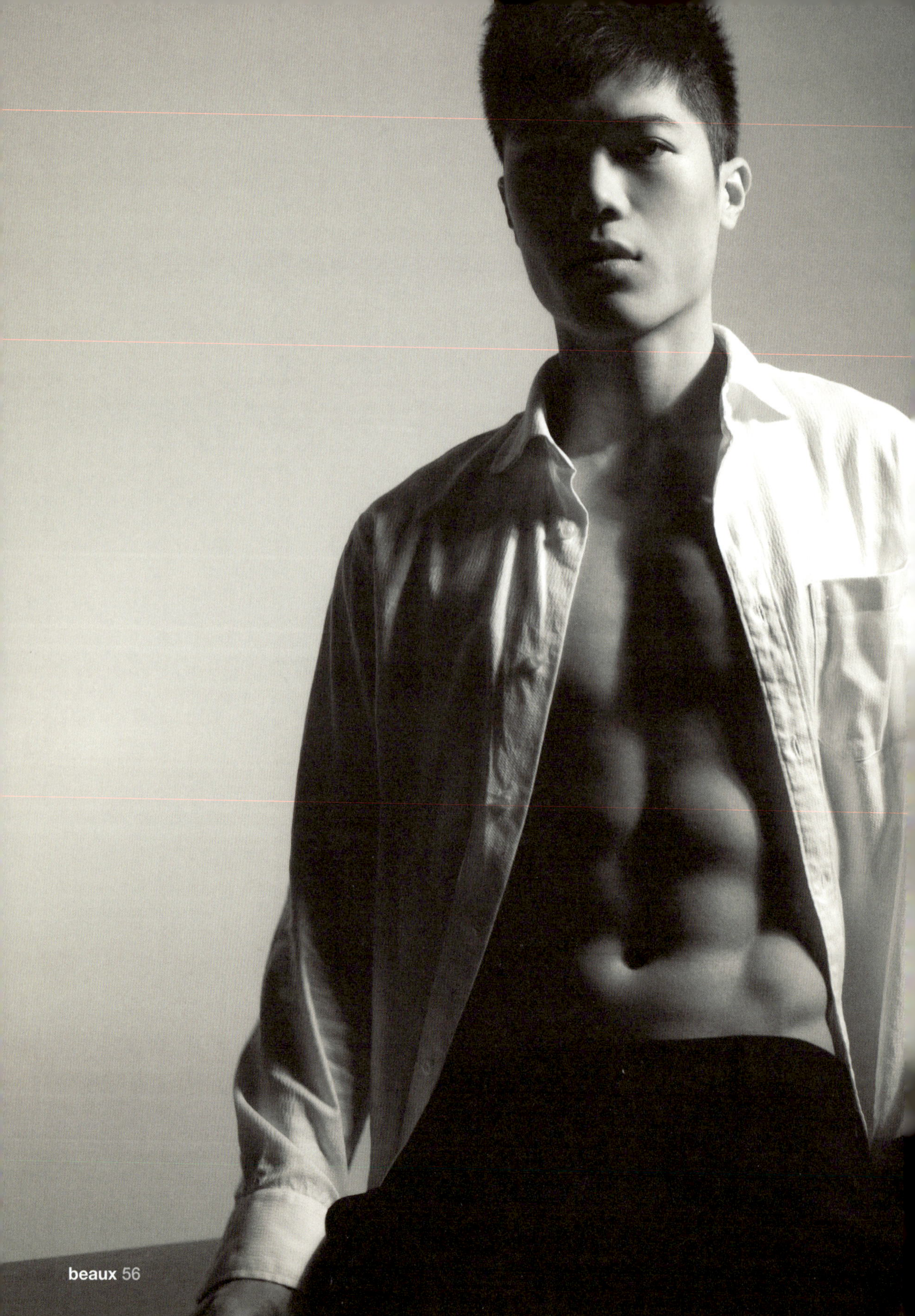

"Vanity and pride are different things, though the words are often used synonymously. A person may be proud without being vain. Pride relates more to our opinion of ourselves, vanity to what we would have others think of us."

Jane Austen
Pride and Prejudice

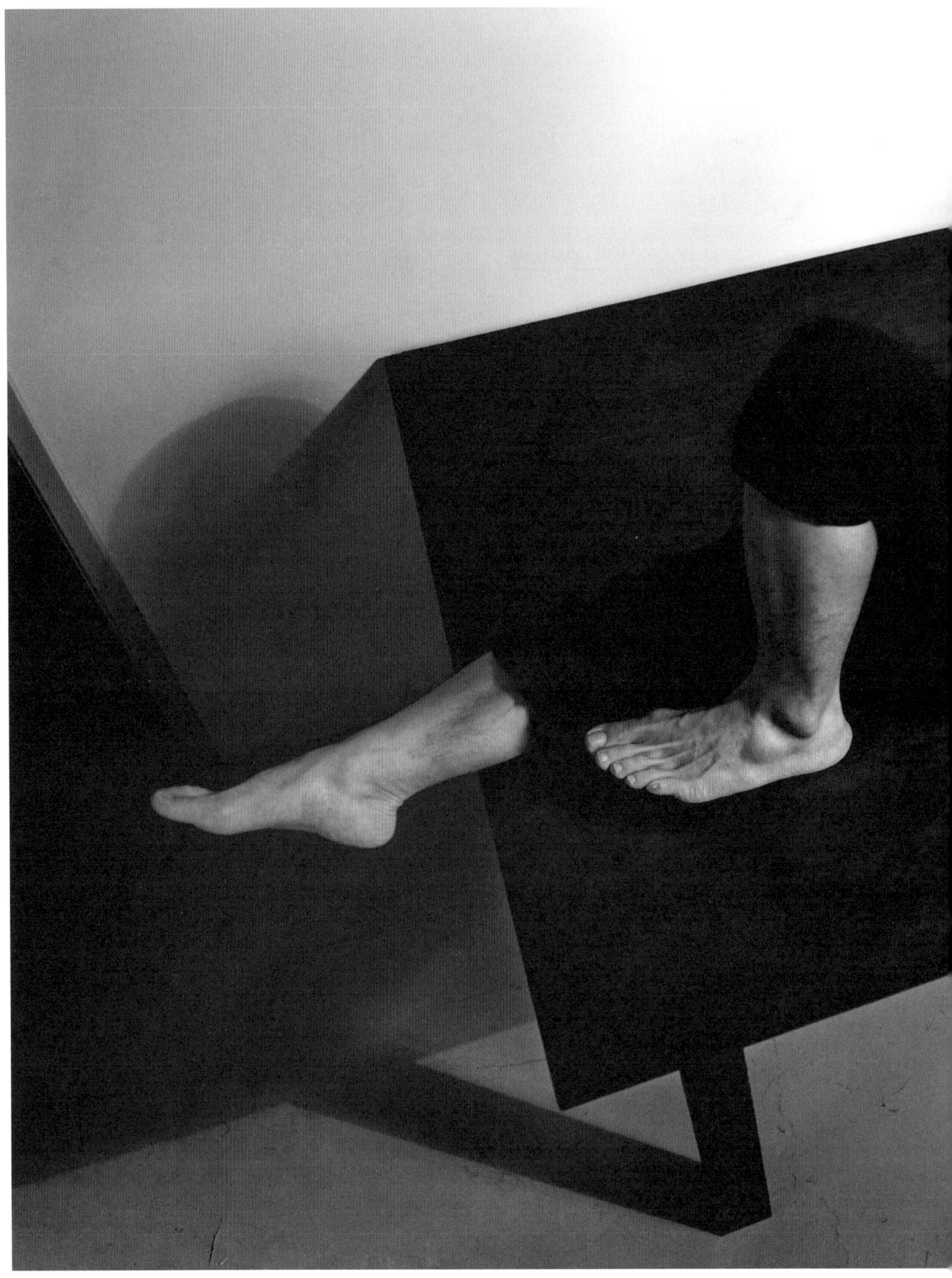

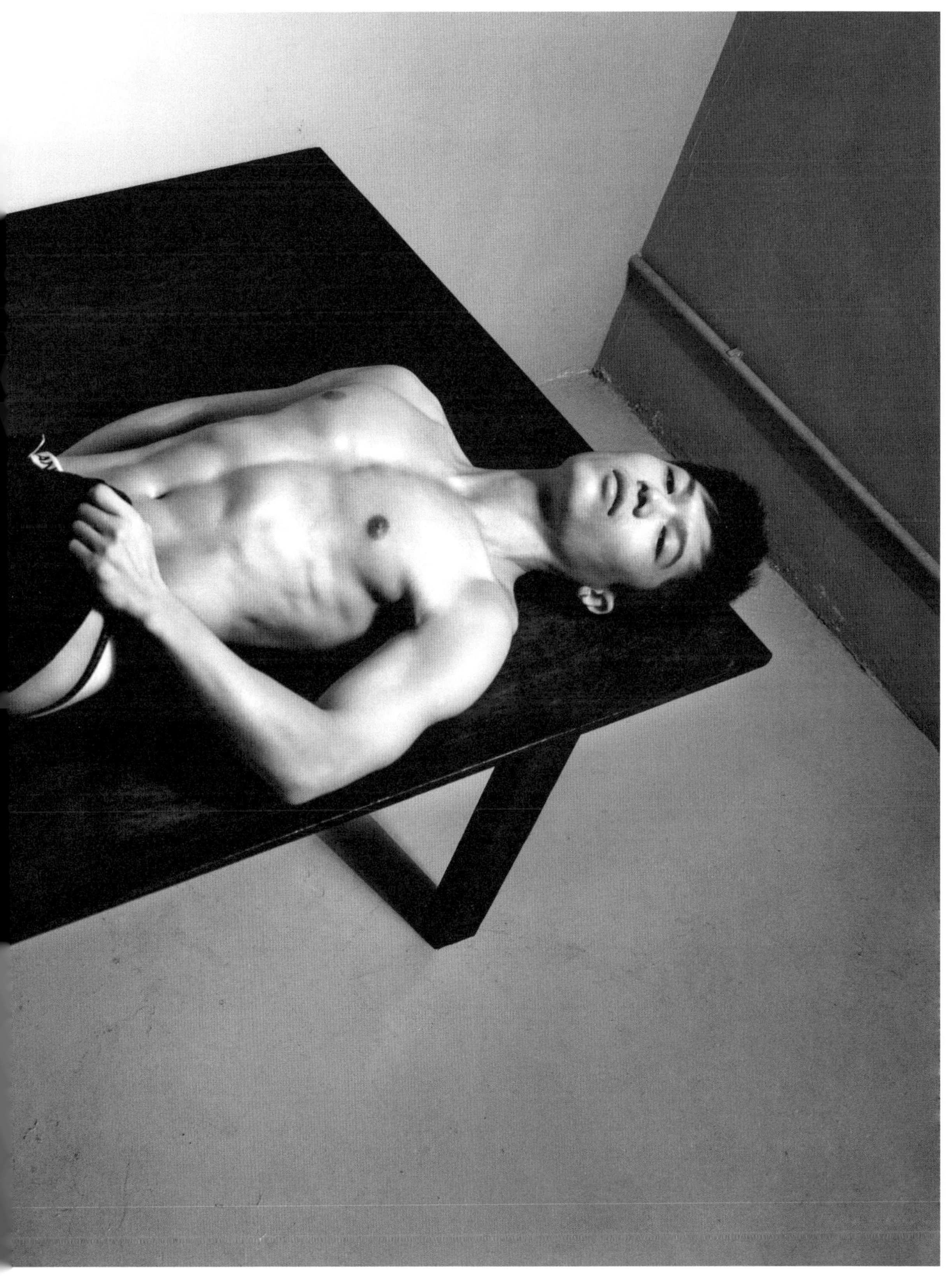

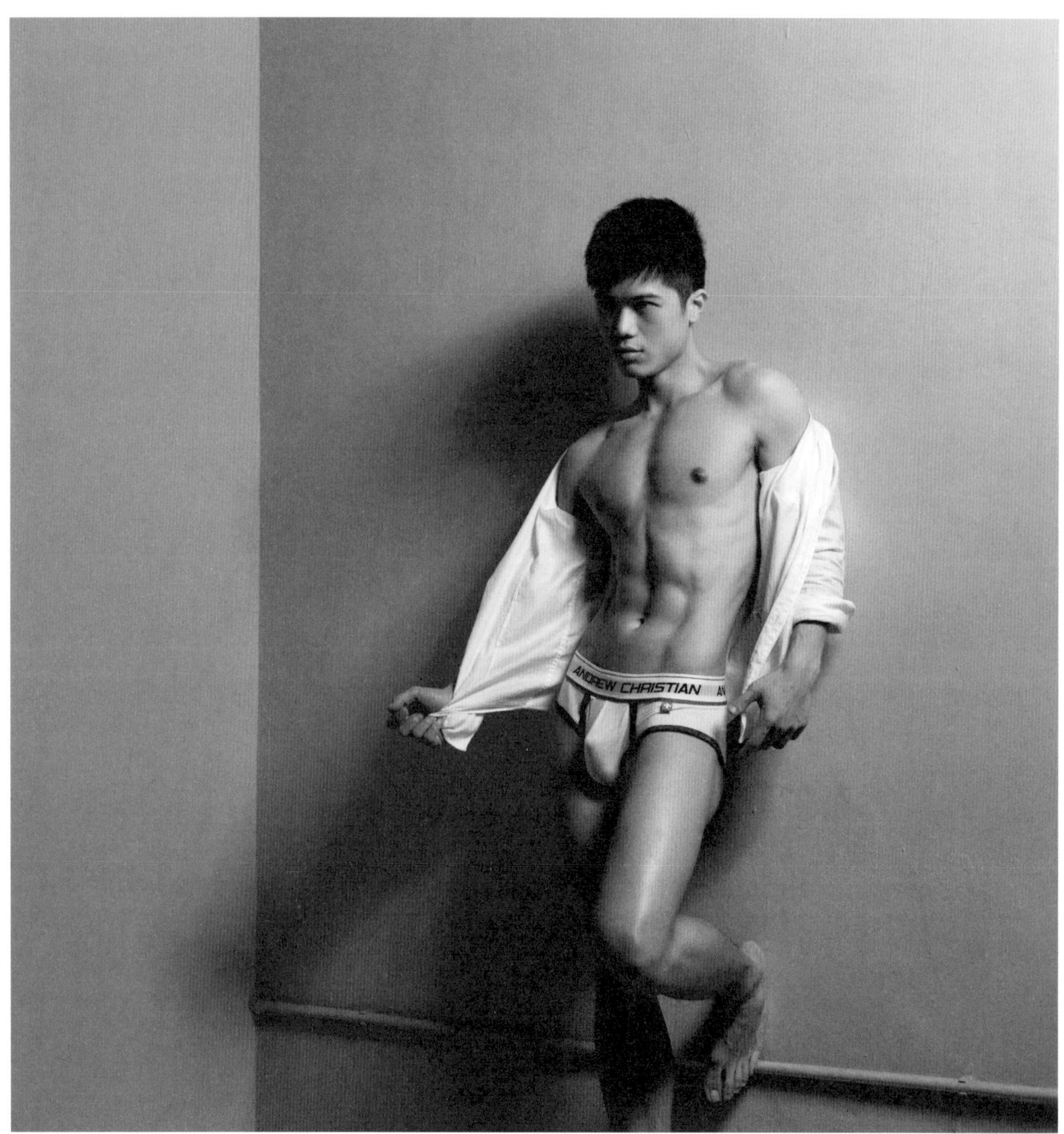
ANDREW CHRISTIAN

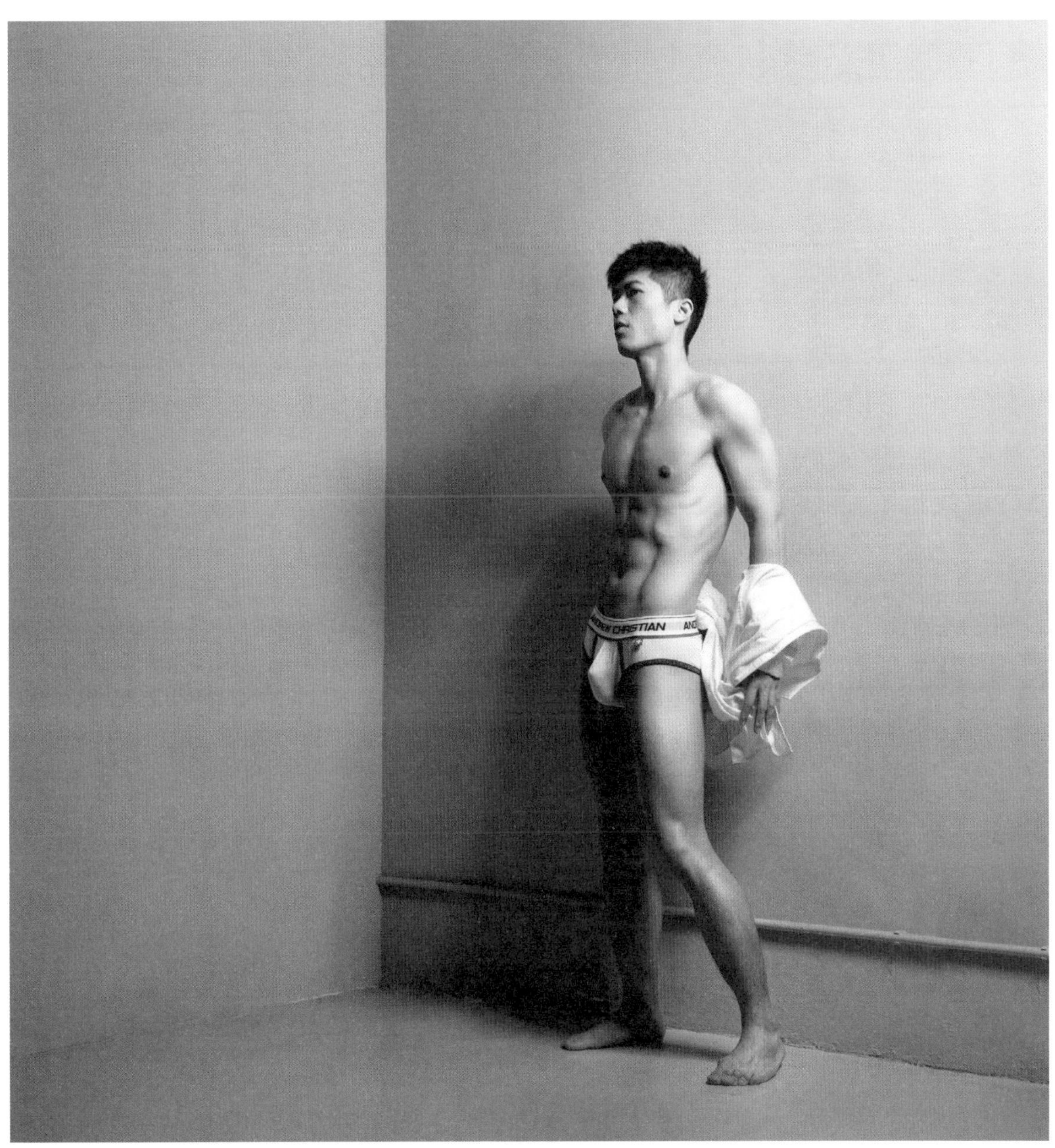

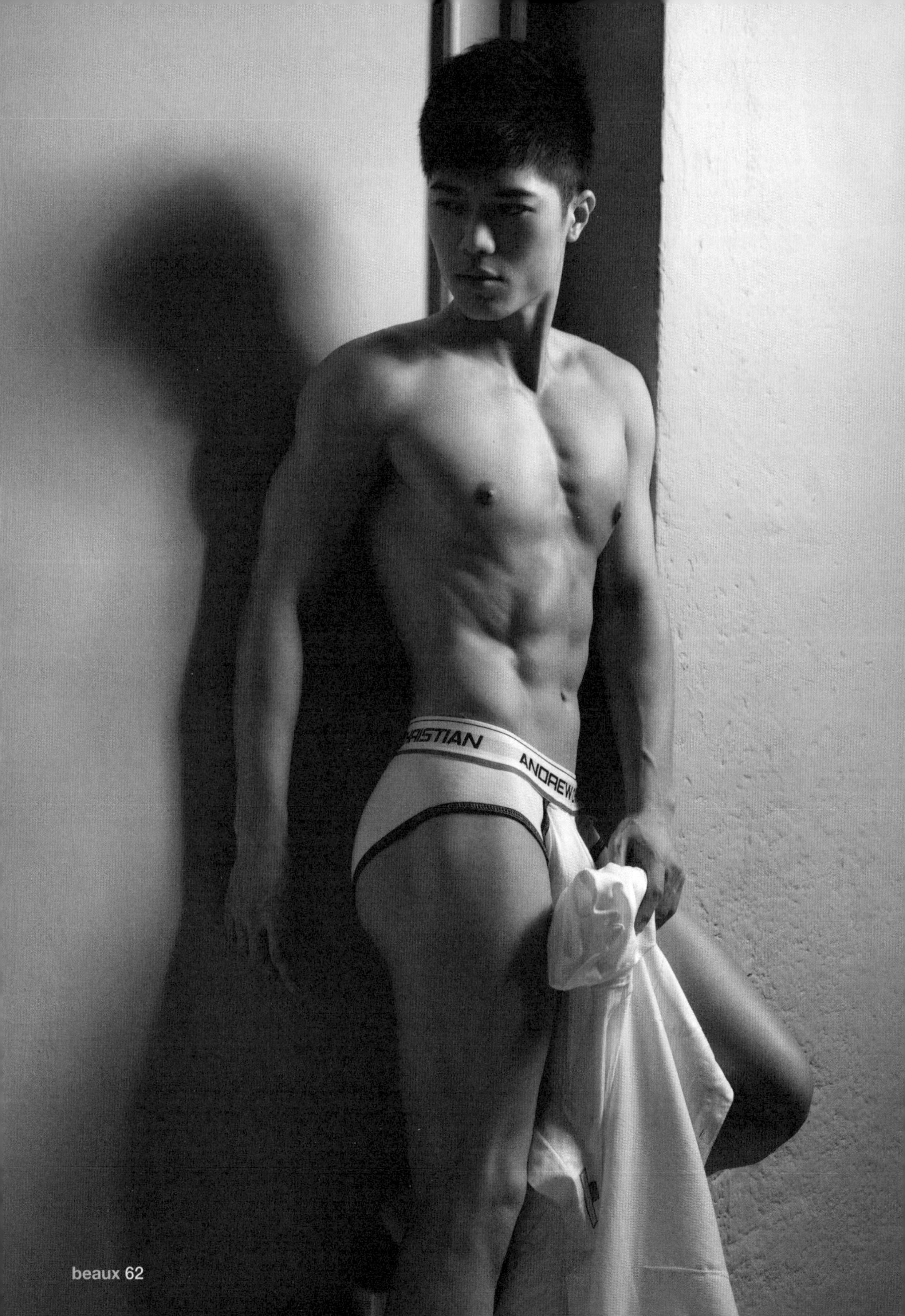
RISTIAN
ANDREW

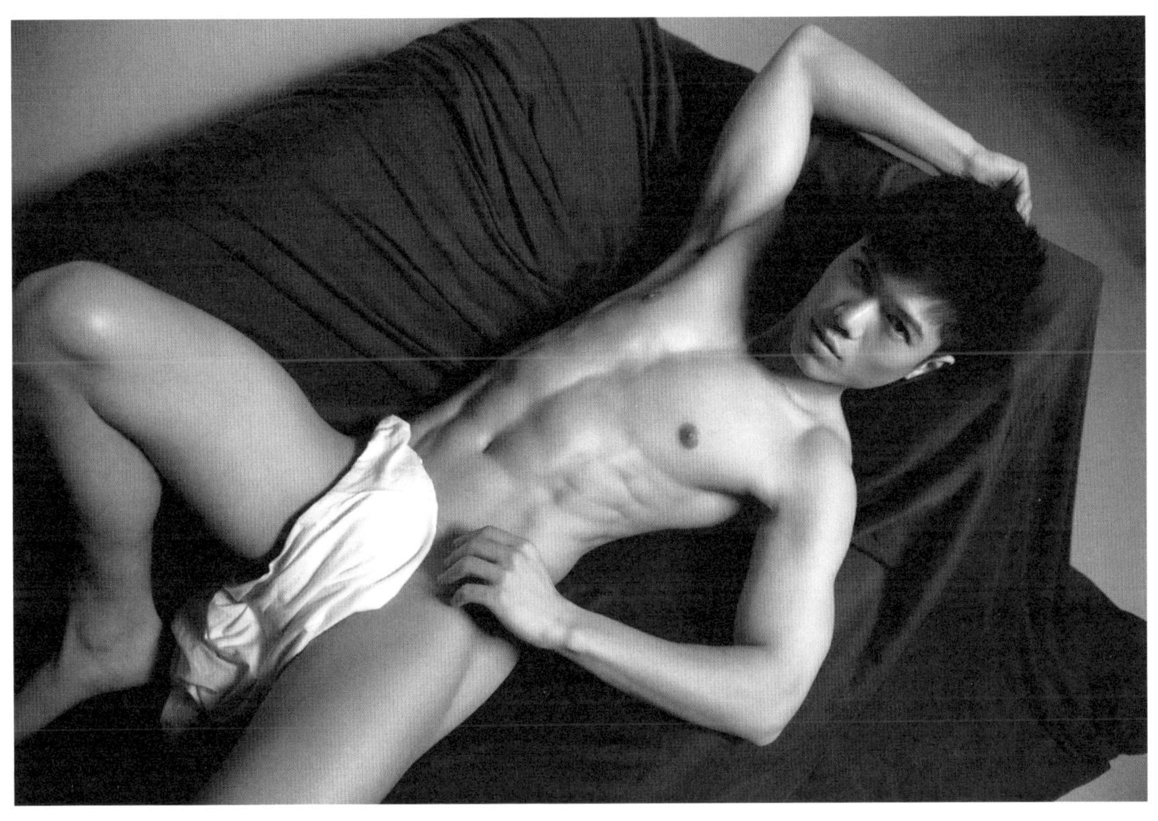

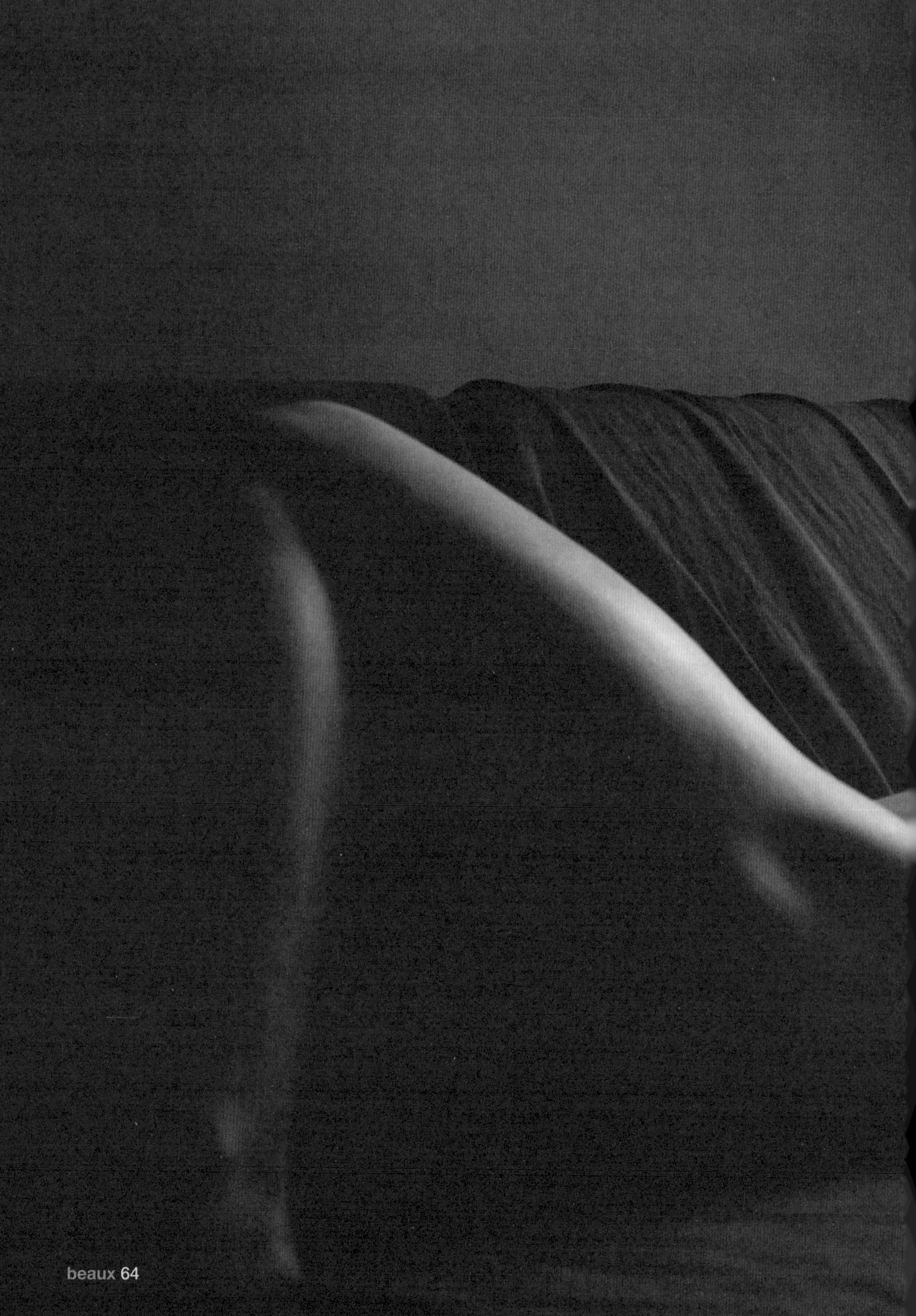

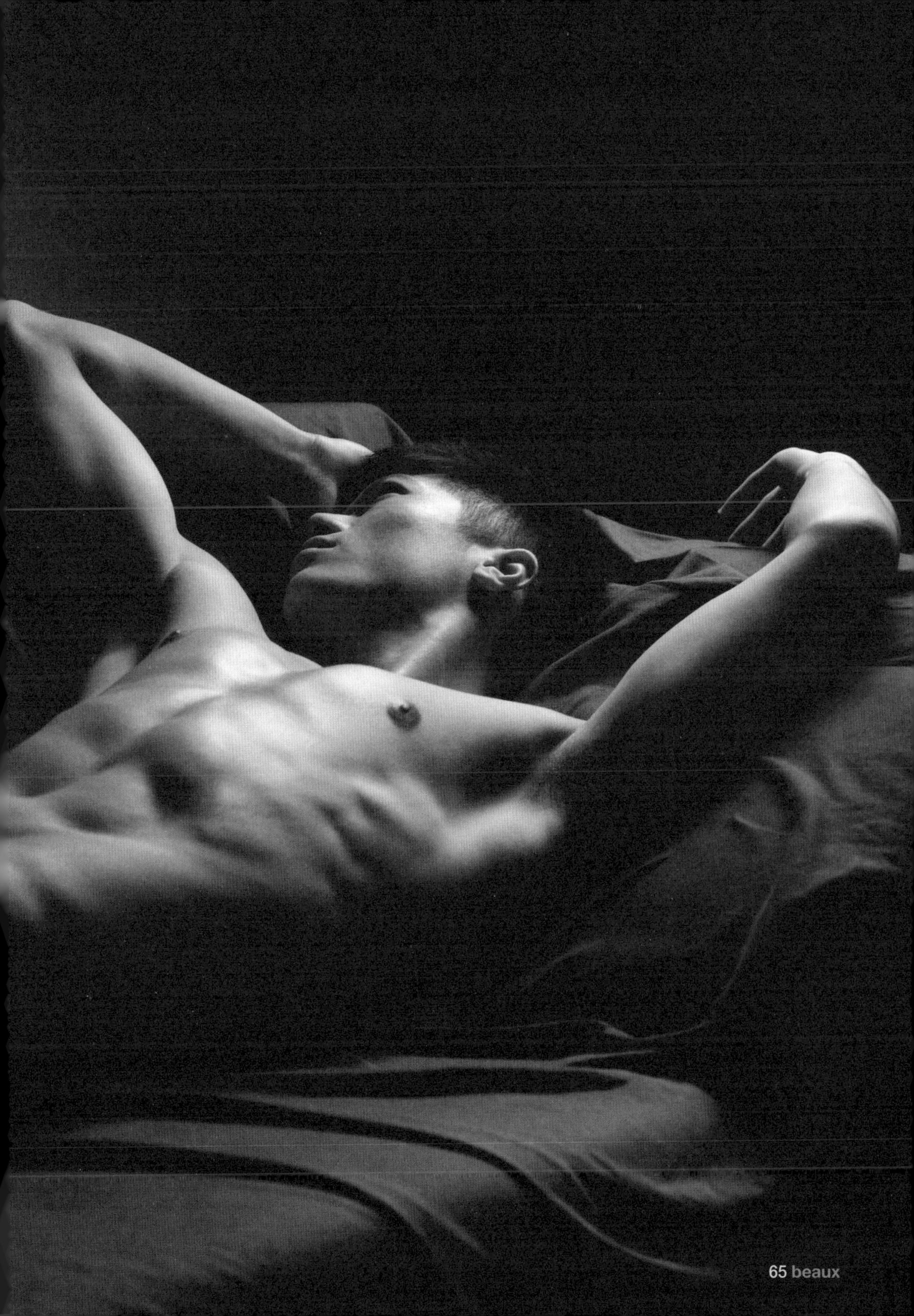

spirit

memory & inspiration

by norm yip; edited by leroy luar

Can you recall some of your earliest memories? People have been known to shell out lots of money for regressive therapy to unearth their deepest memories – some of them a result of experience, others a result of nothing more than deeply held desires and dreams. I need no such assistance. I remember with vivid clarity a dream I once had; a dream of being squeezed through a narrow, uncomfortable space. Breathing was all but impossible and I recall the welcome relief of my return to wakefulness.

Could it be perhaps that this dream is a memory of being in my mother's womb? For I have survived, so to speak, that journey into the world I now live in. I continue to harbour childhood memories of prairies days and endless night skies. I continue to think that there is something more out there; we just haven't found them, or they haven't found us.

Who doesn't remember looking at cloud formations, seeing things appear and disappear before your very eyes – people, animals, monsters, fantasies. For this exercise in imagination and perception, the sky's literally the limit.

I remember sitting in the back seat of the family station wagon, scratching fleeting symbols of wonder and mystery upon the frost on the car window. They are, without a doubt, simply one of my fondest memories - my greatest gift of inspiration. They are uniquely mine. But they are not mine alone because everything is connected together by forces we are only beginning to understand in our Universe.

This is the Spirit in which my art presides.

All artwork shown in the ***spirit*** *section are available for sale unless otherwise noted.*
For more information, contact us at ***enquiry@beauxmagazine.com****.*

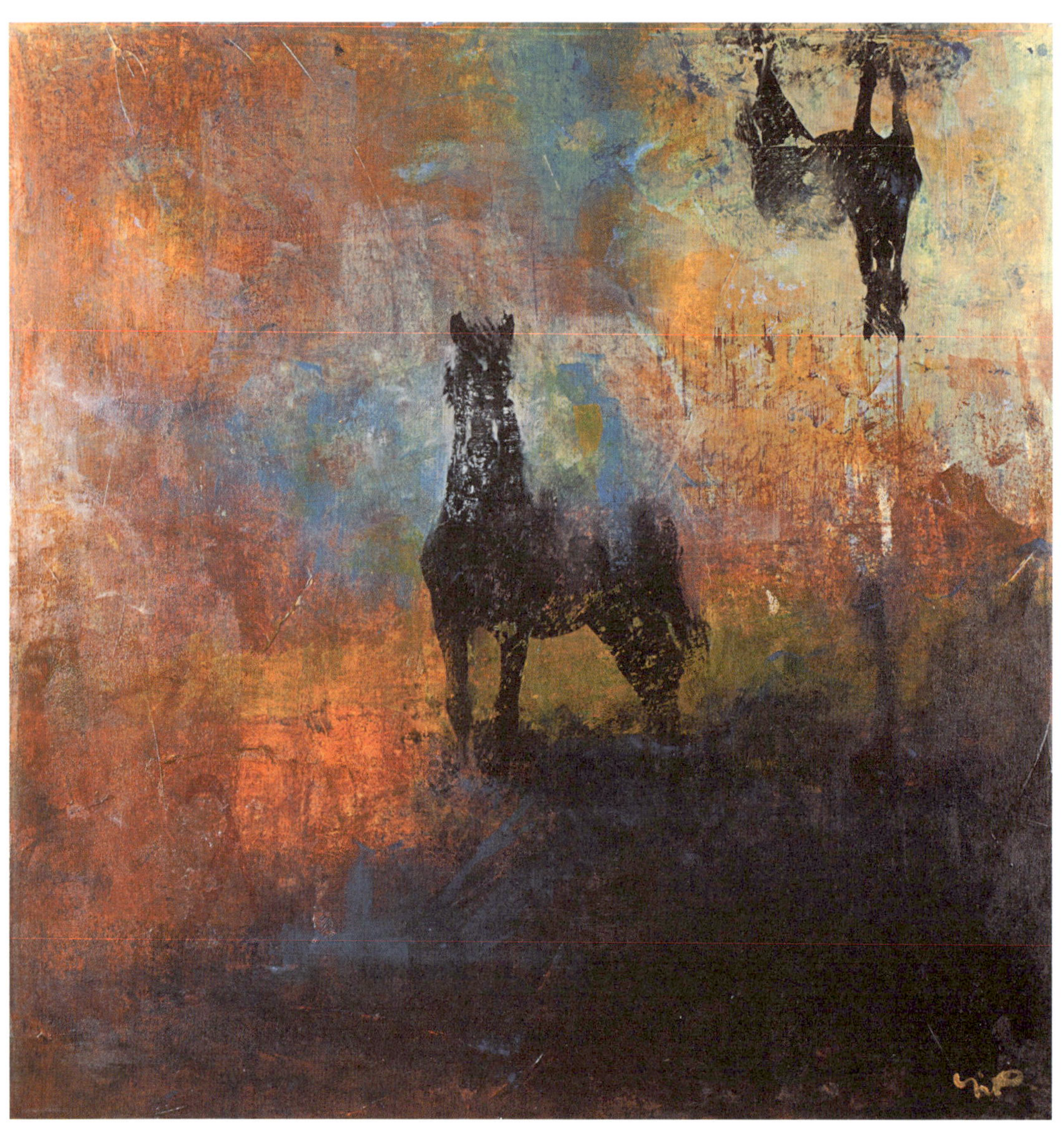

Pride by Norm Yip, 2012
Photography, acrylic and dye transfer on wood. 1000 x 1000mm.
Private collection.

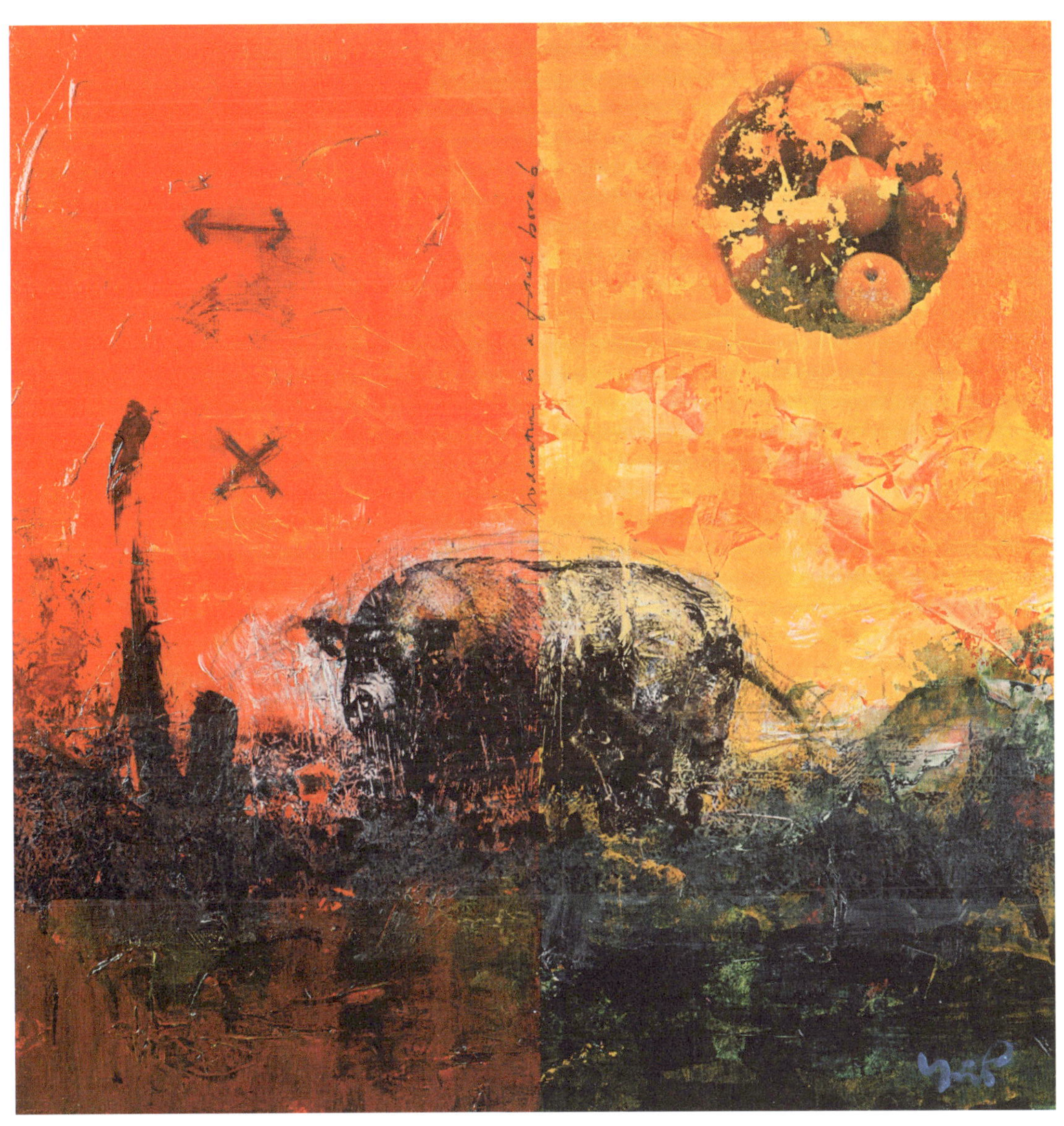

Gluttony by Norm Yip, 2012
Photography, acrylic and dye transfer on wood.
600 x 600mm.

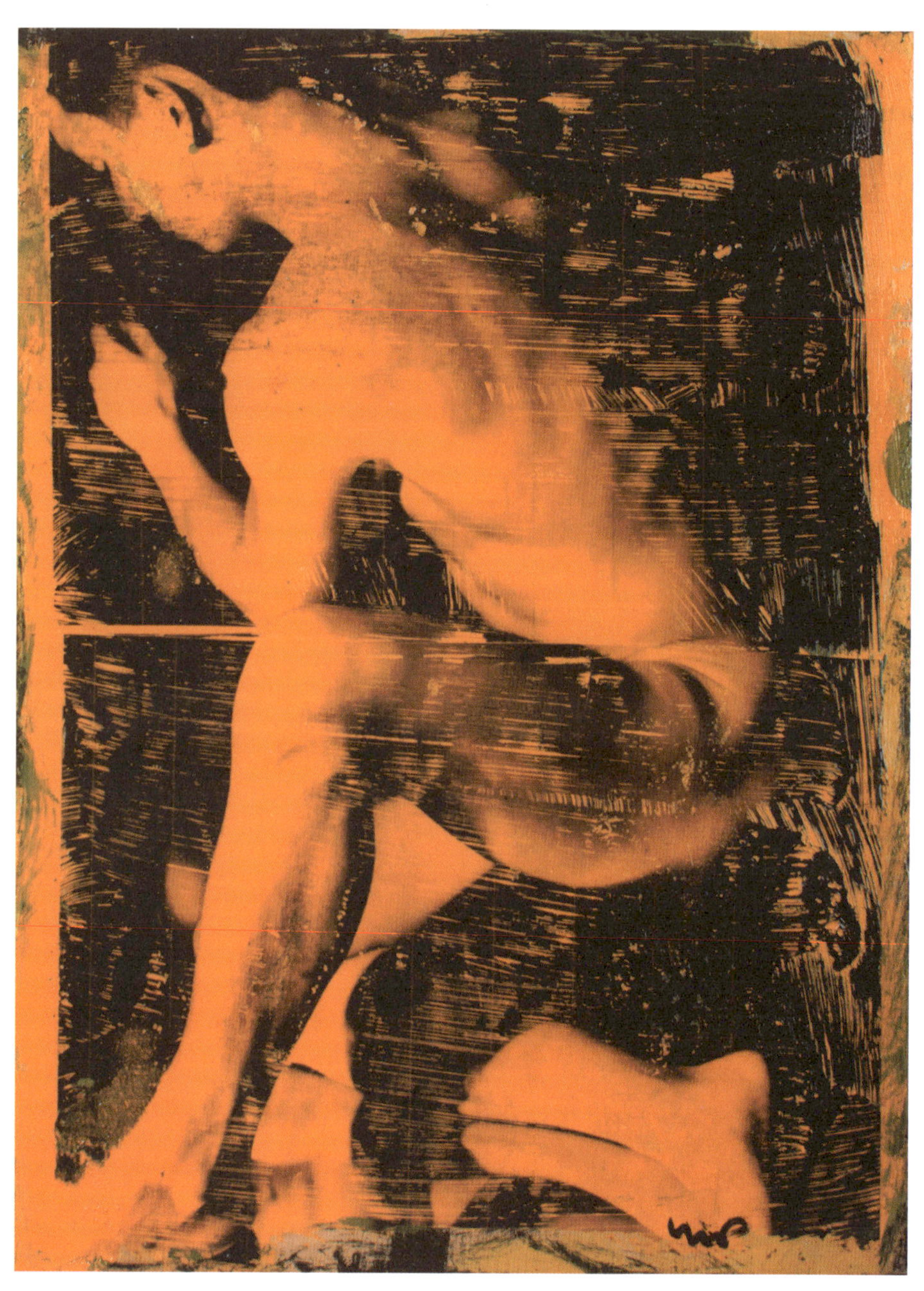

Narcissist by Norm Yip, 2012
Photography, acrylic and dye transfer on wood.
300 x 400mm.

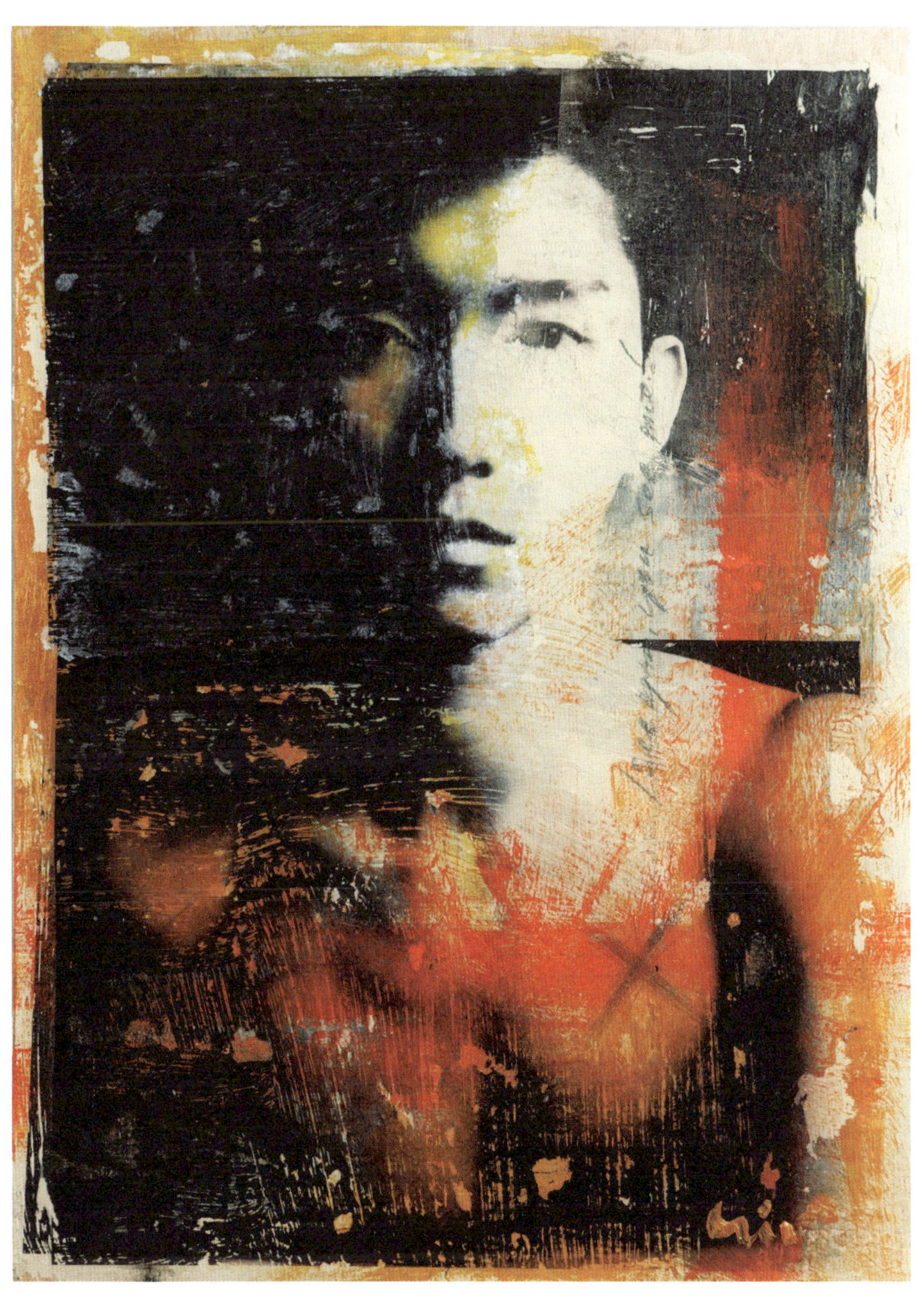

I see you; you see me by Norm Yip, 2012
Photography, acrylic and dye transfer on wood.
300 x 400mm.

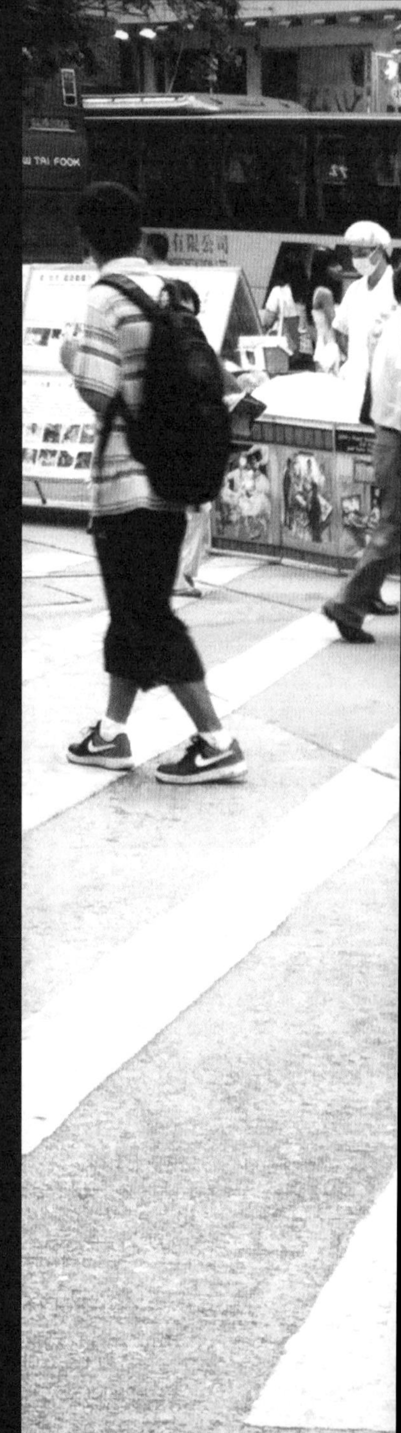

Take a Picture, It'll Last Longer

by Norm Yip

Don't say you haven't tried it, we know you have. How often have you seen someone you were simply dying to take a photograph of? With our mobile devices increasingly performing at a level on par with the best photography technology, anyone can be a street photographer on the go and an inconspicuous one at that.

In Hong Kong, everyone is a street photographer and the best thing about it is that it's completely legal – as long as you don't cause a commotion, of course. Nothing could be simpler; spot your subject, approach downwind, a quick, furtive snap and you're on your way and he's on his.

How your street photography comes out also depends largely on your approach. You could be guerrilla about it or you could march up to your subject full-on. Be warned however as this sport isn't without its risks. Only if you're a seasoned expert or possess exceptional bravado should you attempt to photograph your subject's face close-up. And woe betide you should you forget to disable your auto-flash.

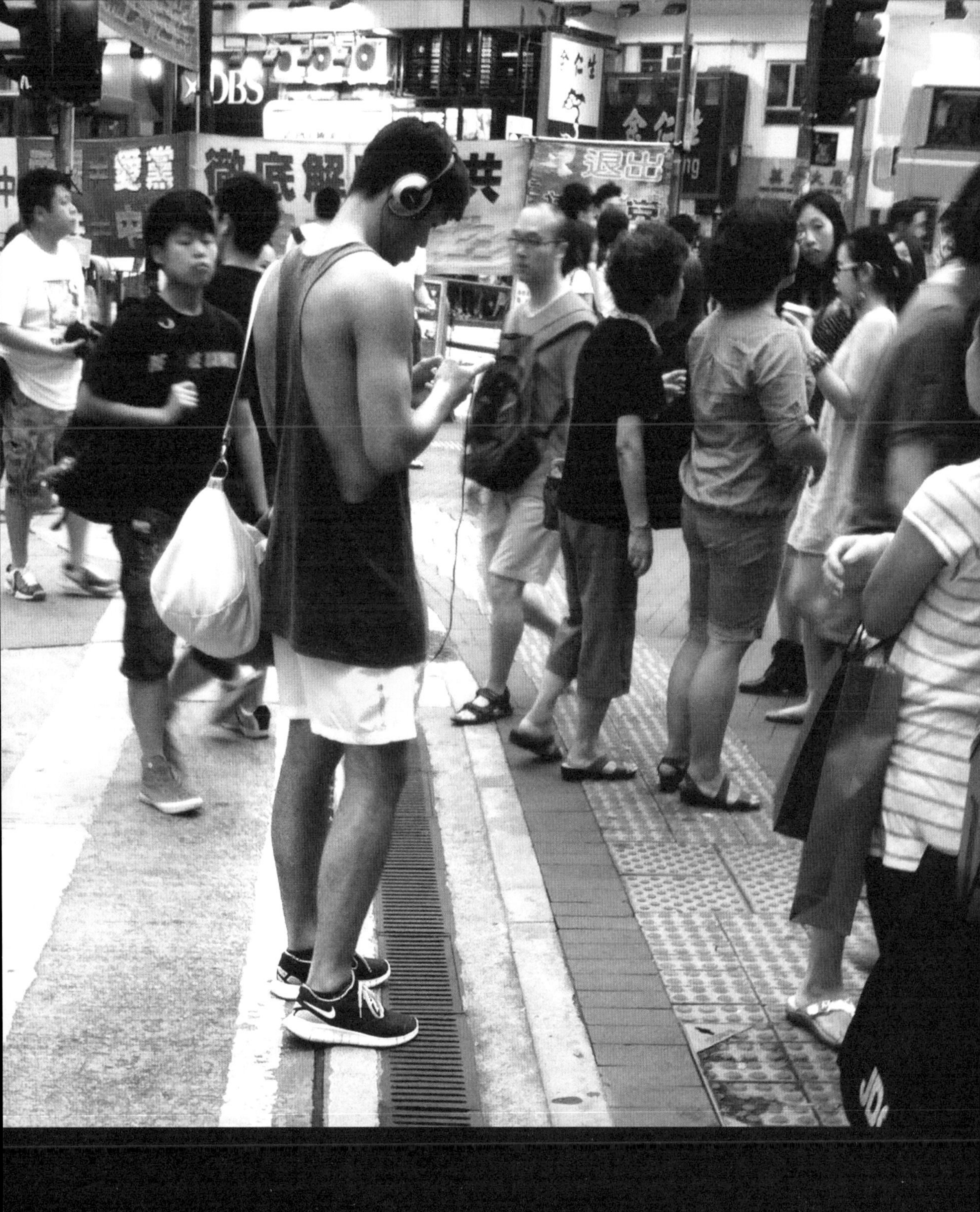
DBS
徹底解
退出

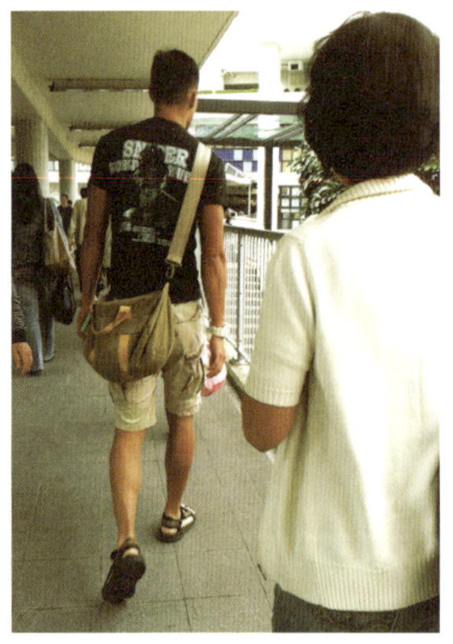

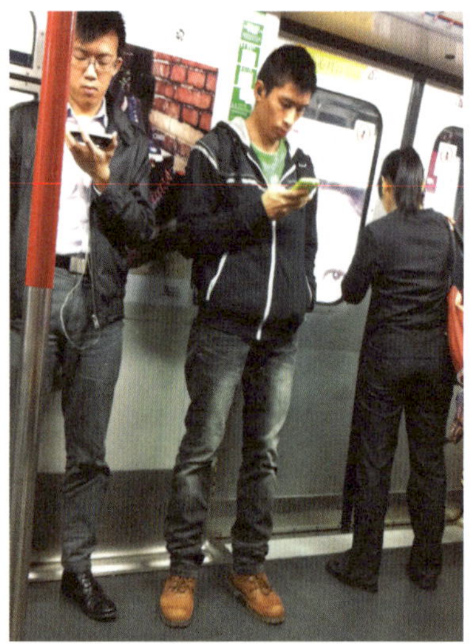

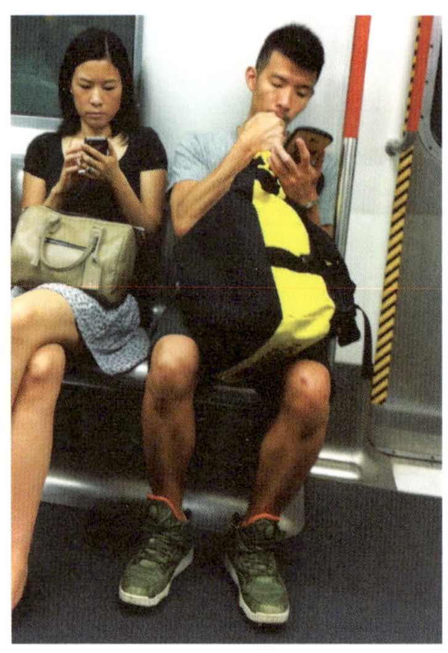

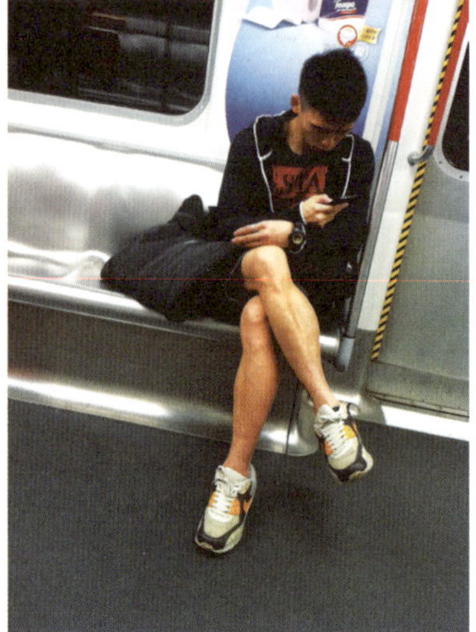

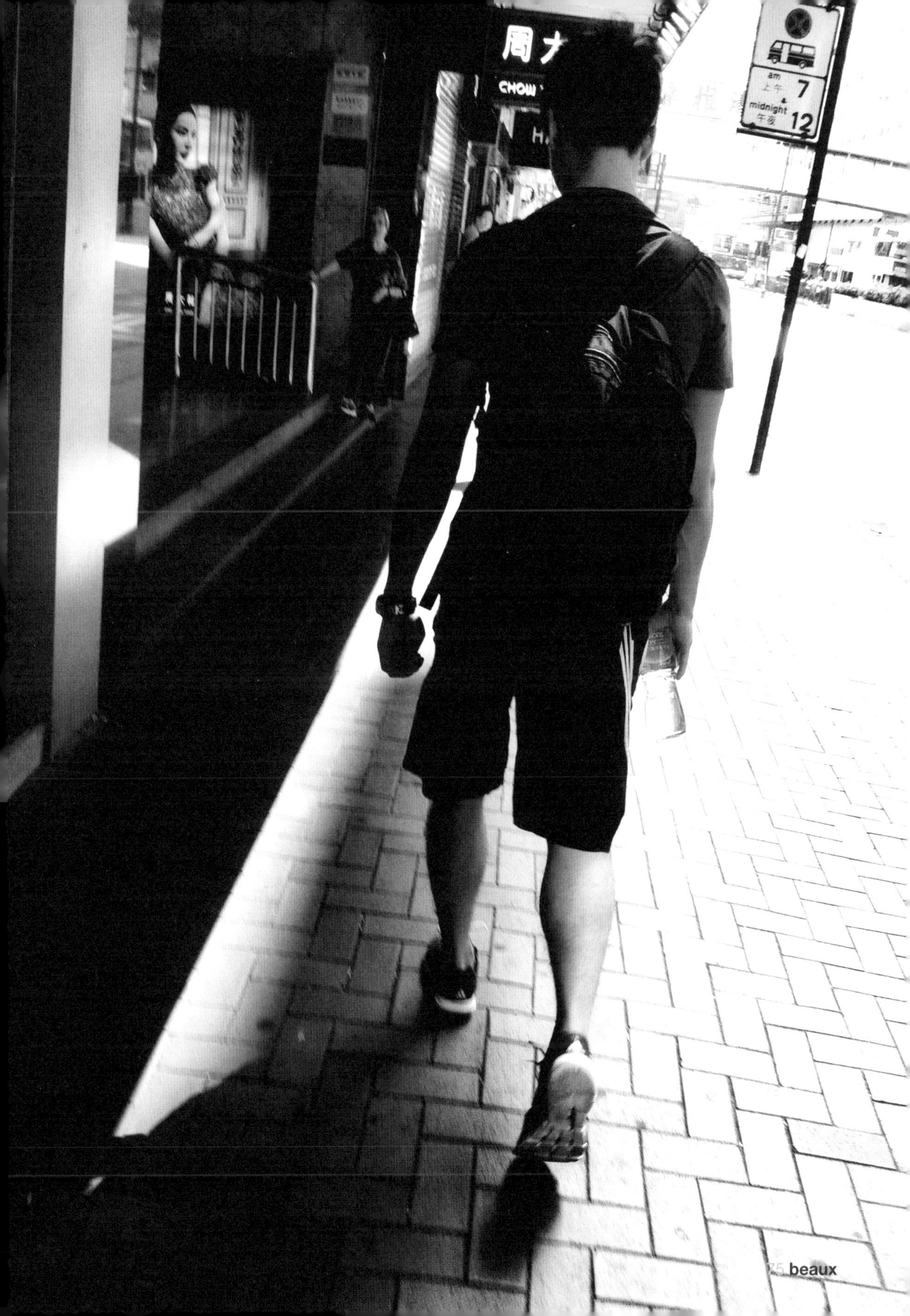
周大
CHOW
am
上午
7
midnight
午夜
12

The streets of Hong Kong are a mecca for street photography. While beauxspotting is all about capturing the beauty of unsuspecting Asian men, street photography is also about capturing fleeting moments in time; the kissing couple, the weary street dog, the wise alley cat, the predatory taxi – just about anything and everything that holds meaning to the photographer.

We look up to Henri-Cartier Bresson, his compact Leica rangefinder and his philosophy of capturing that split moment in time – his most definitive works beautifully compiled in The Decisive Moment.

In a way, beauxspotting attempts to capture more than just a decisive moment. It is an expression of the hunt for attraction; possibly invasive in that moment of capture but never obscene or predatory. We enjoy the photograph after the fact for its inherent beauty. The image of the young man and his short shorts, Nike runners and deep sleeveless tank-top, as perfect in its innocence and immediacy as it can never be found in a choreographed setting.

Have you been been beauxspotting? Send your image(s) to **submissions@beauxmagazine.com** *with 'beauxspotting' in the subject heading. Your initial images should be at least 150 dpi or higher in resolution. If selected, we will need 300 dpi for printing. In addition, we'll send you a copy of the*

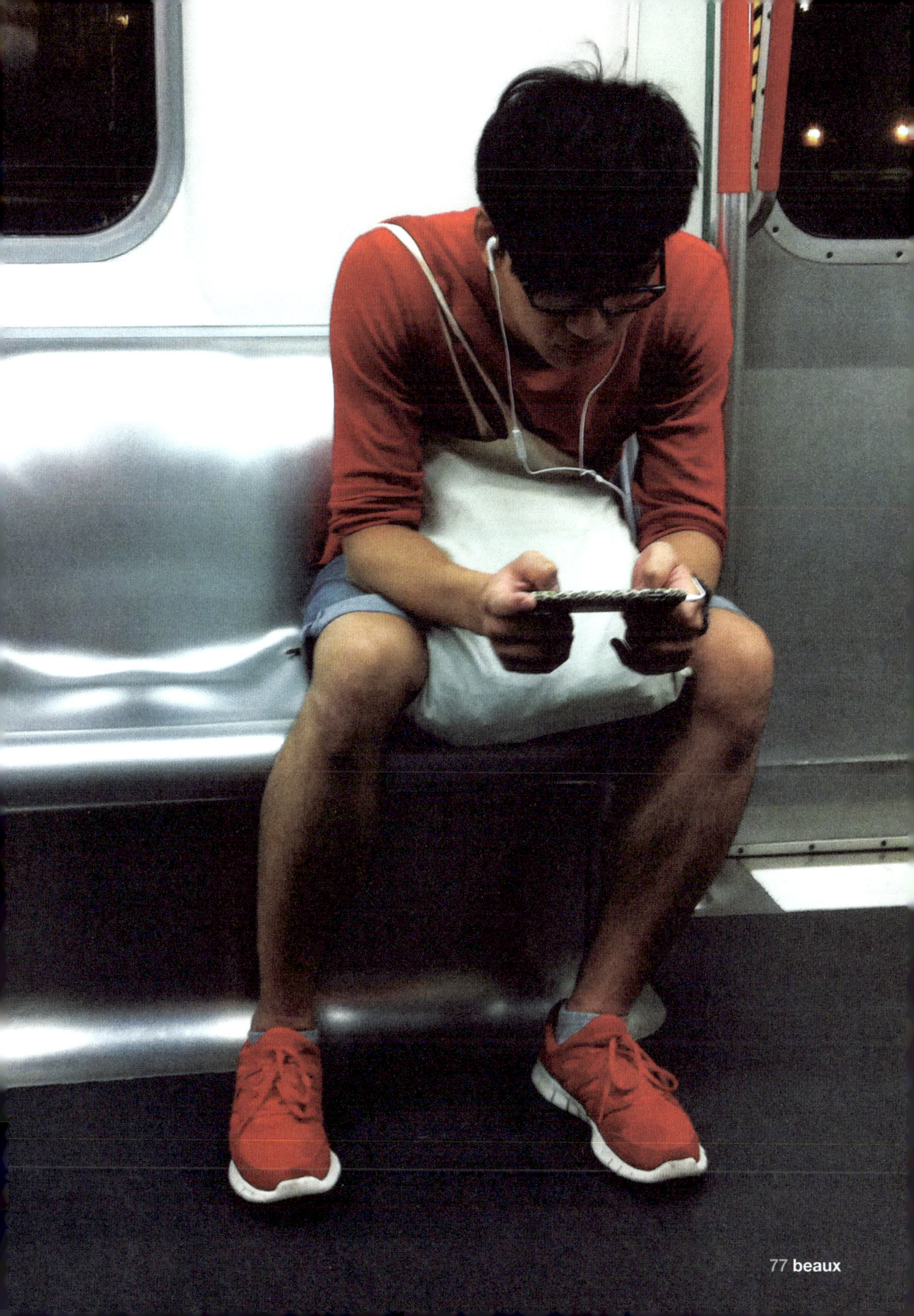

shootout

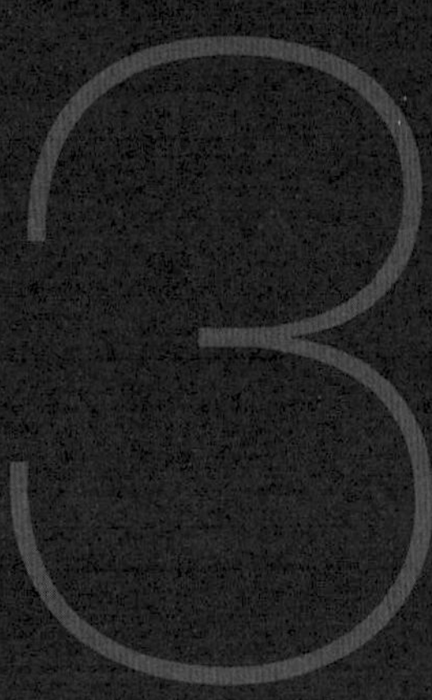

Photographer Norm Yip
Model Loren Tam, Chinese, Hong Kong
Location Courtesy of Larry Ng

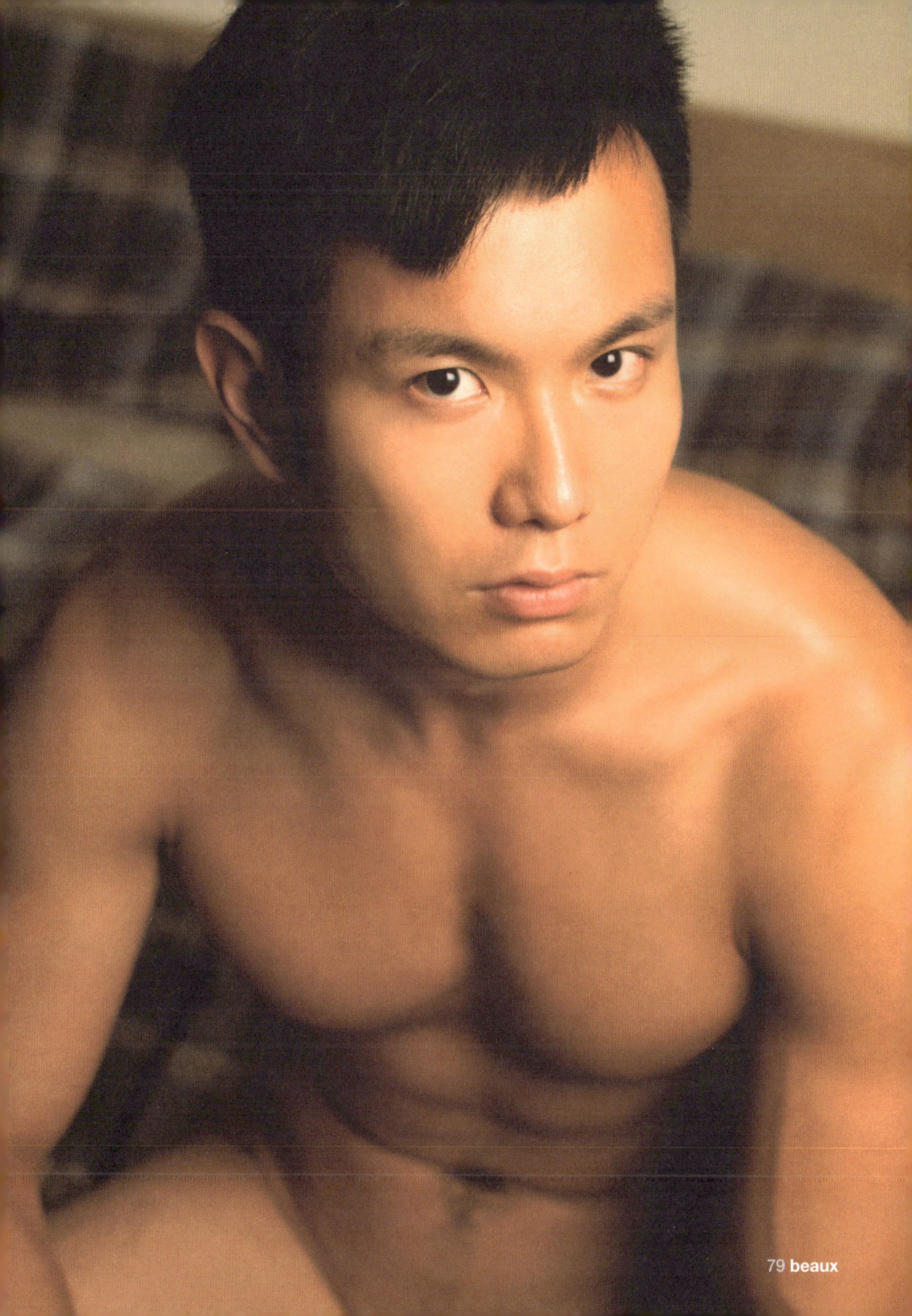

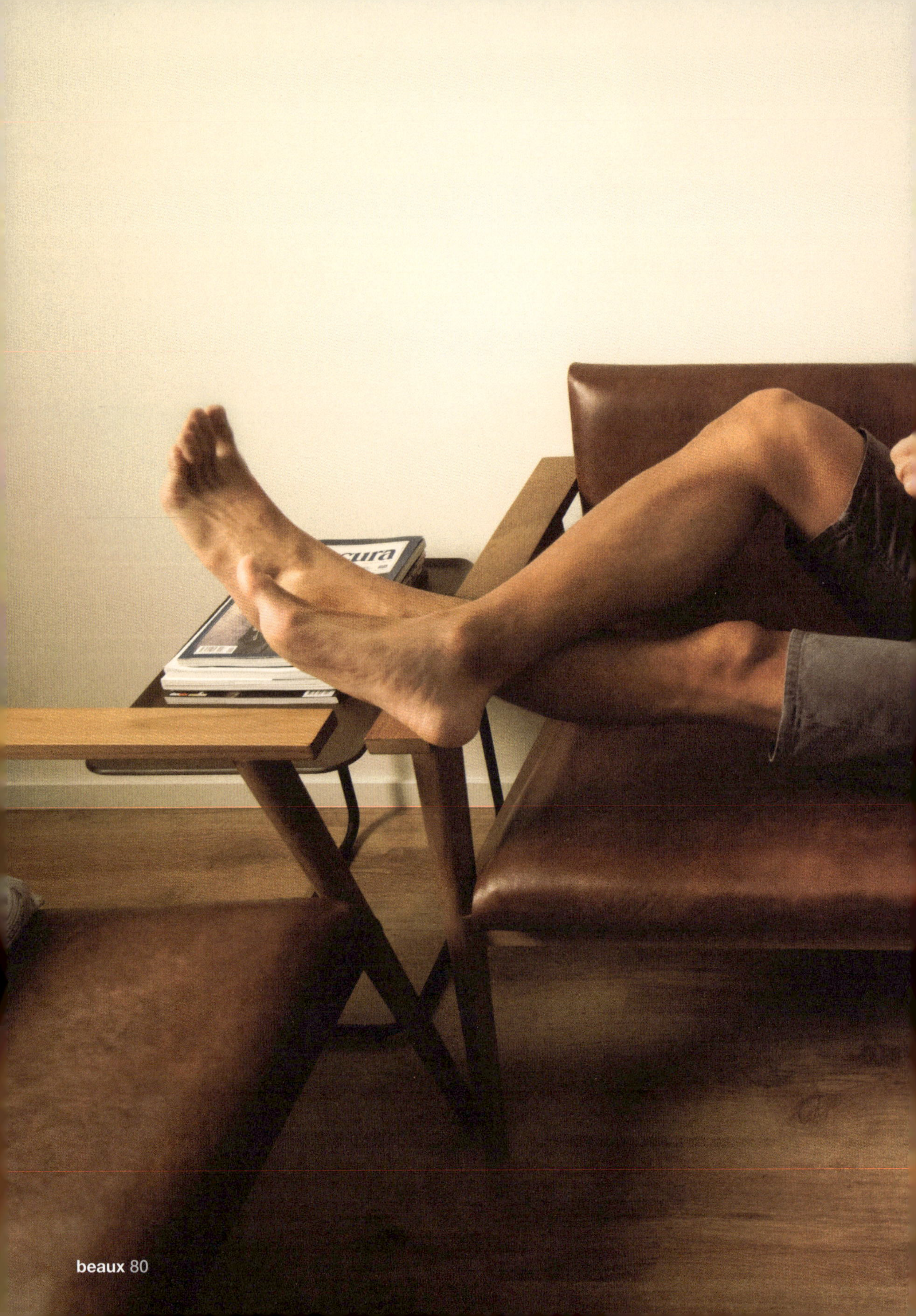

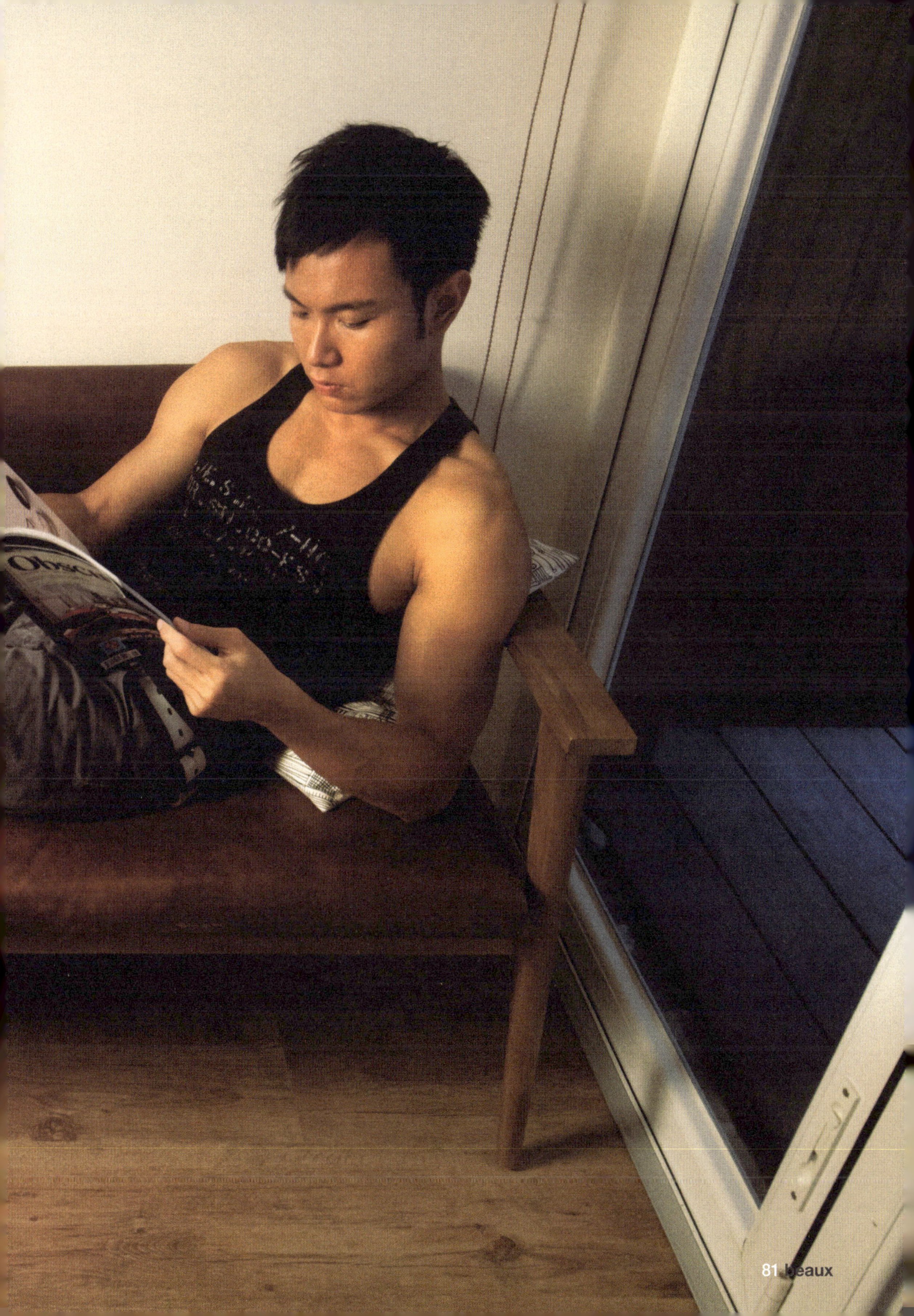

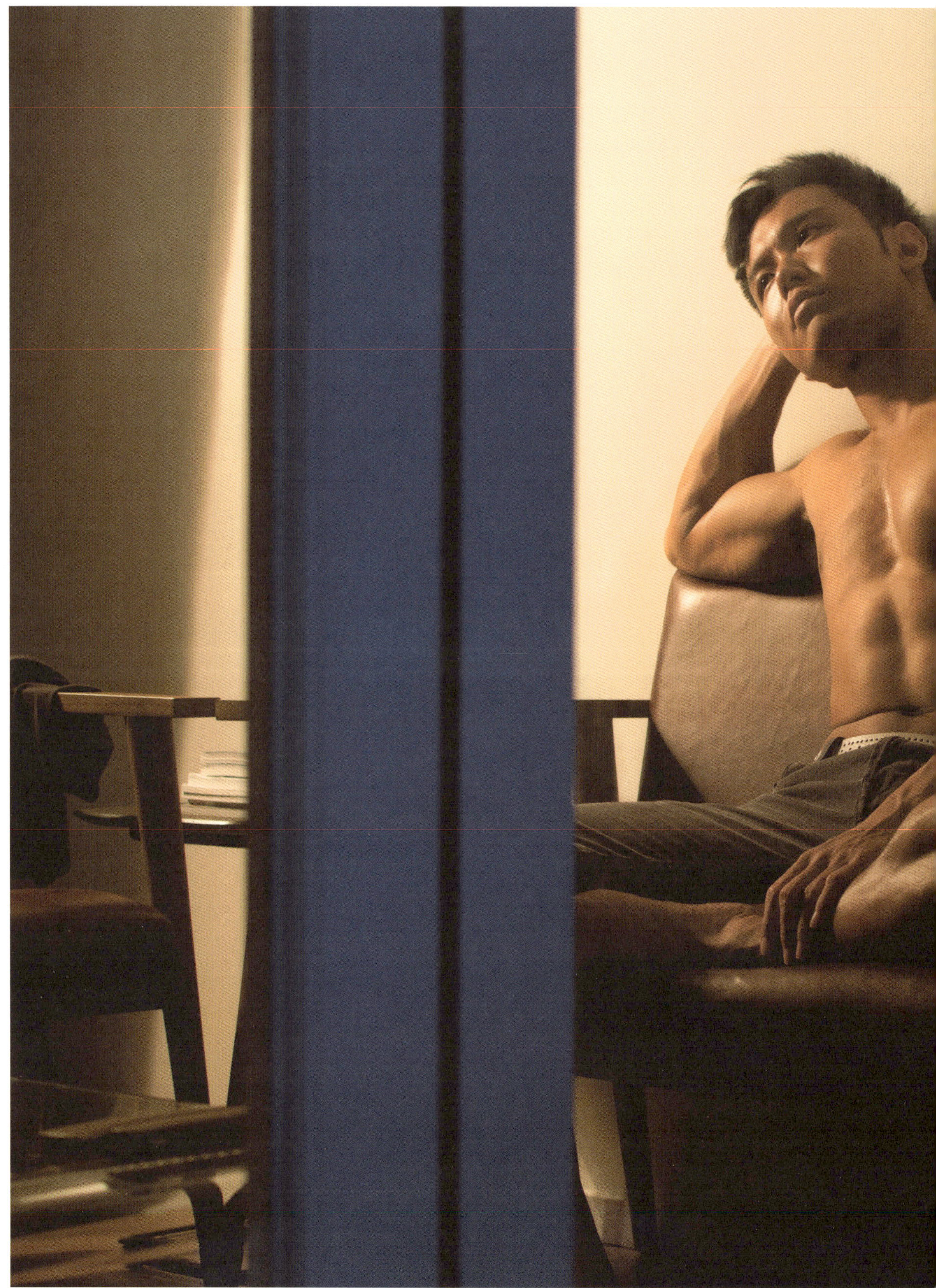

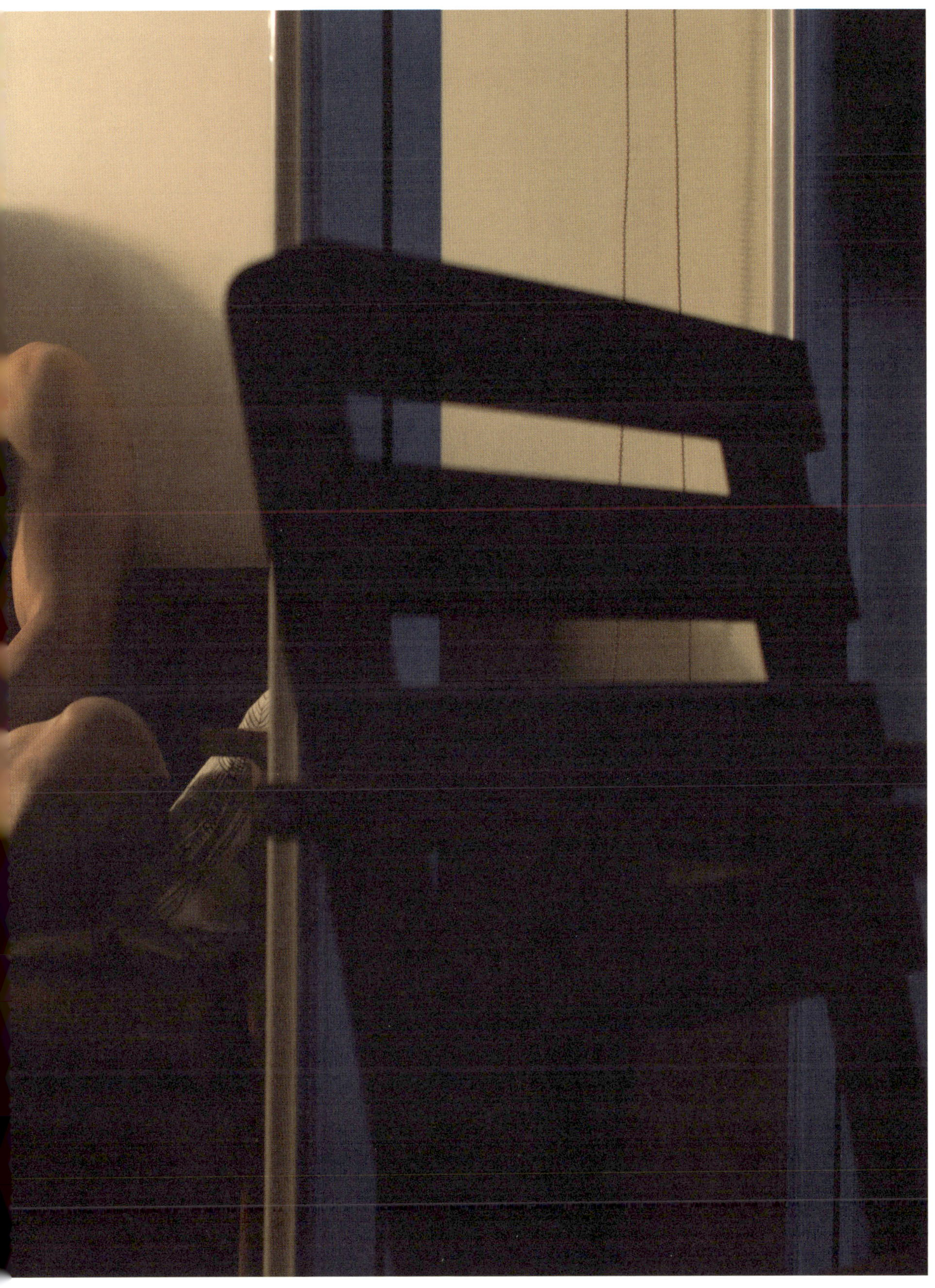

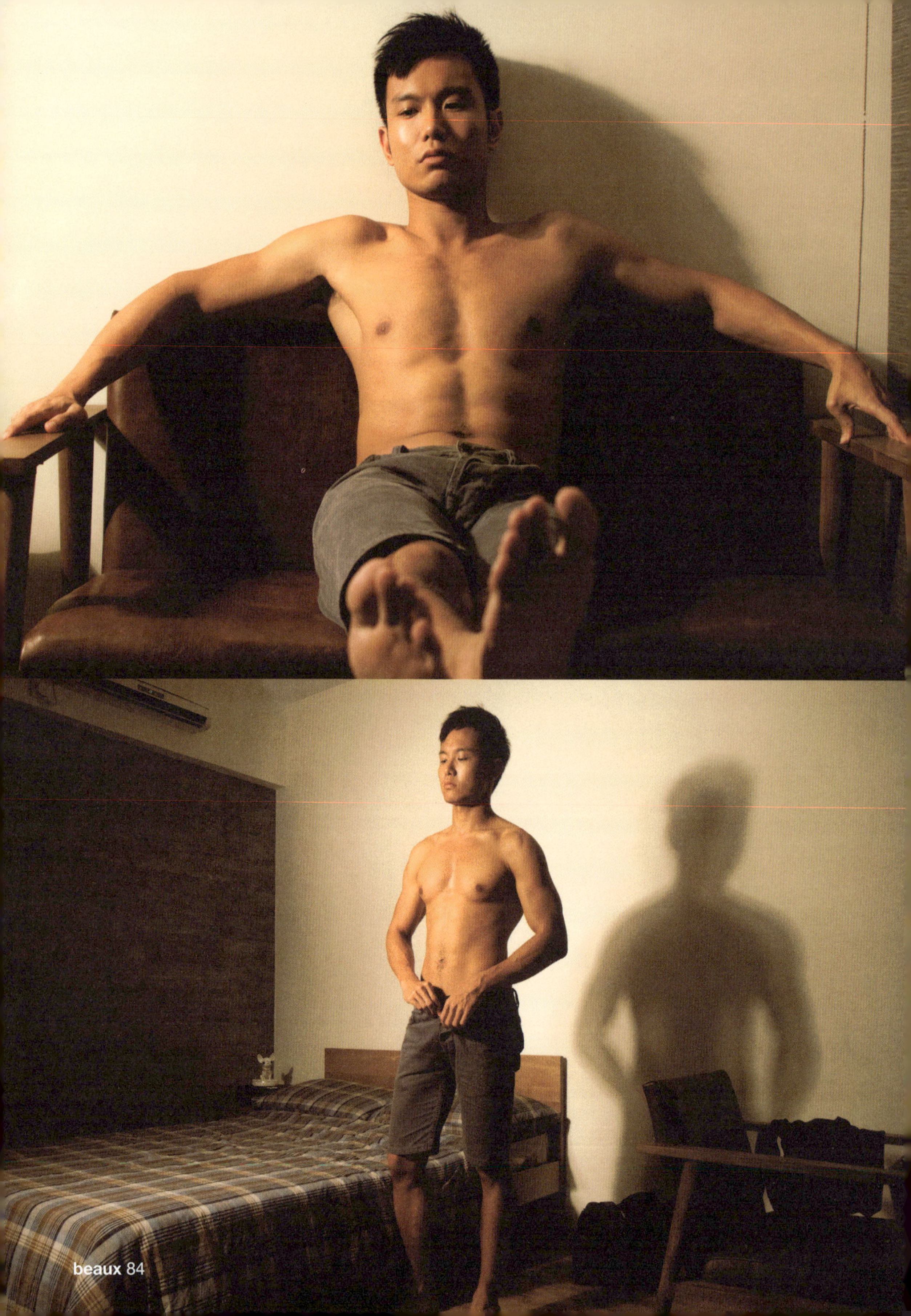

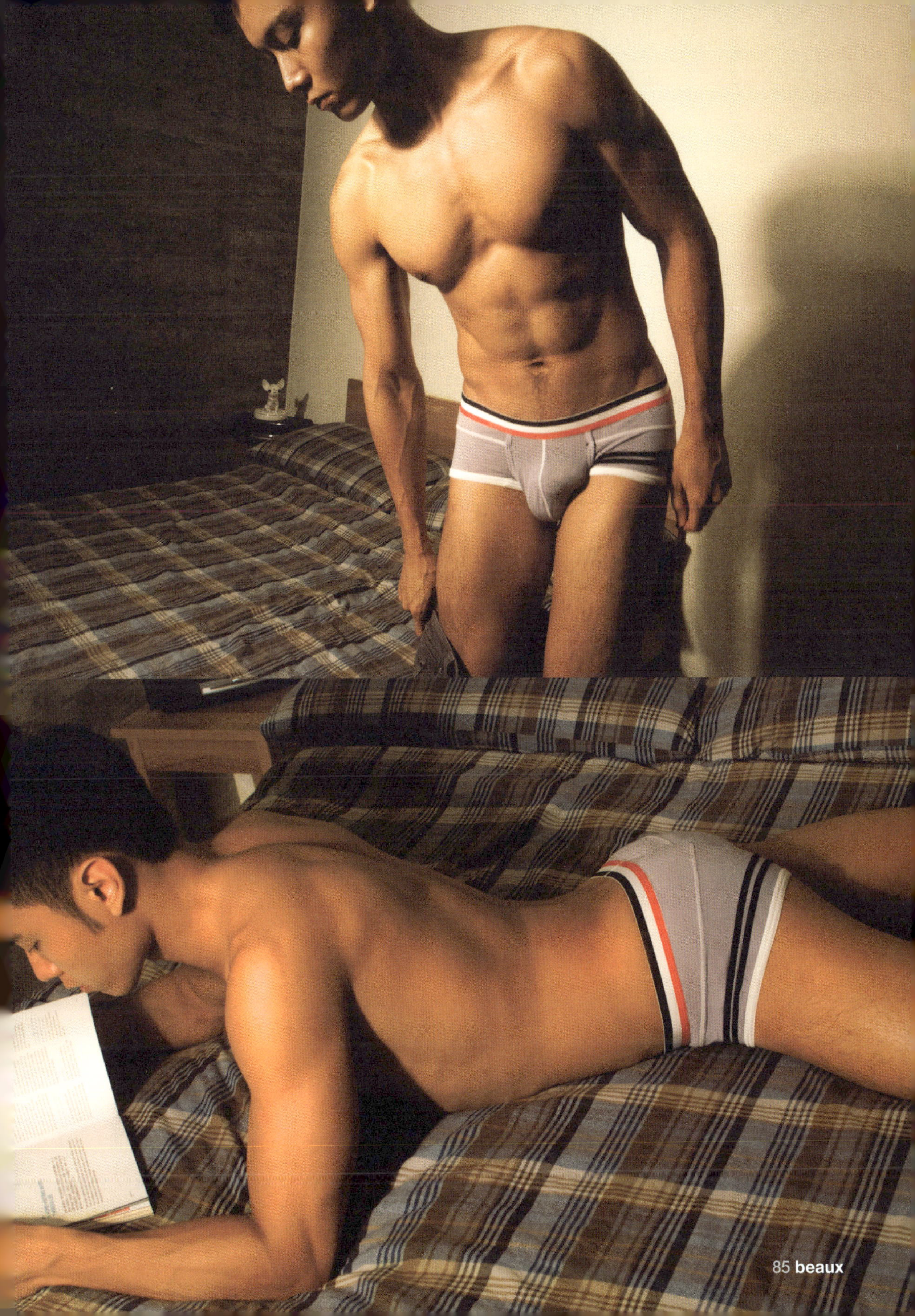

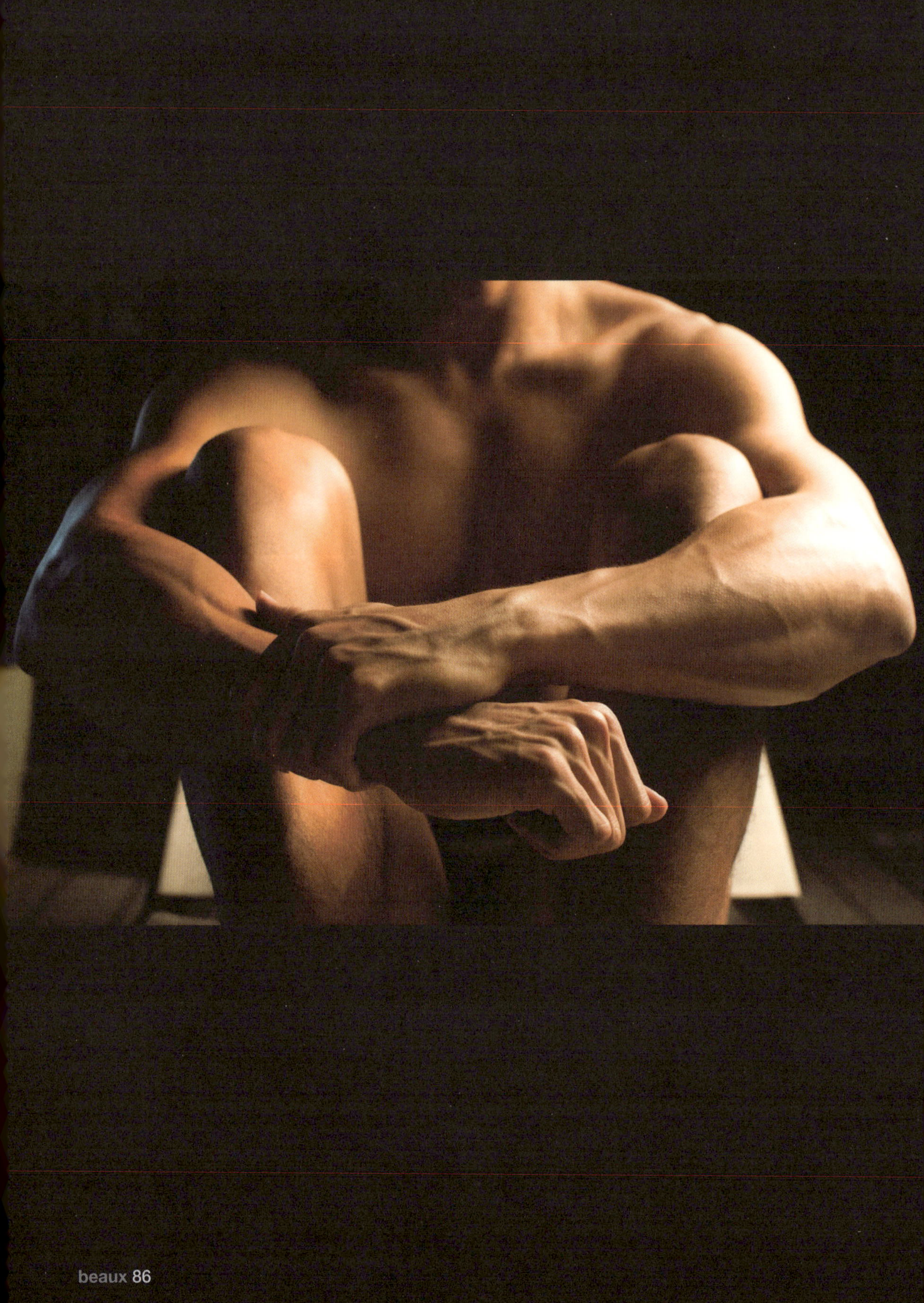

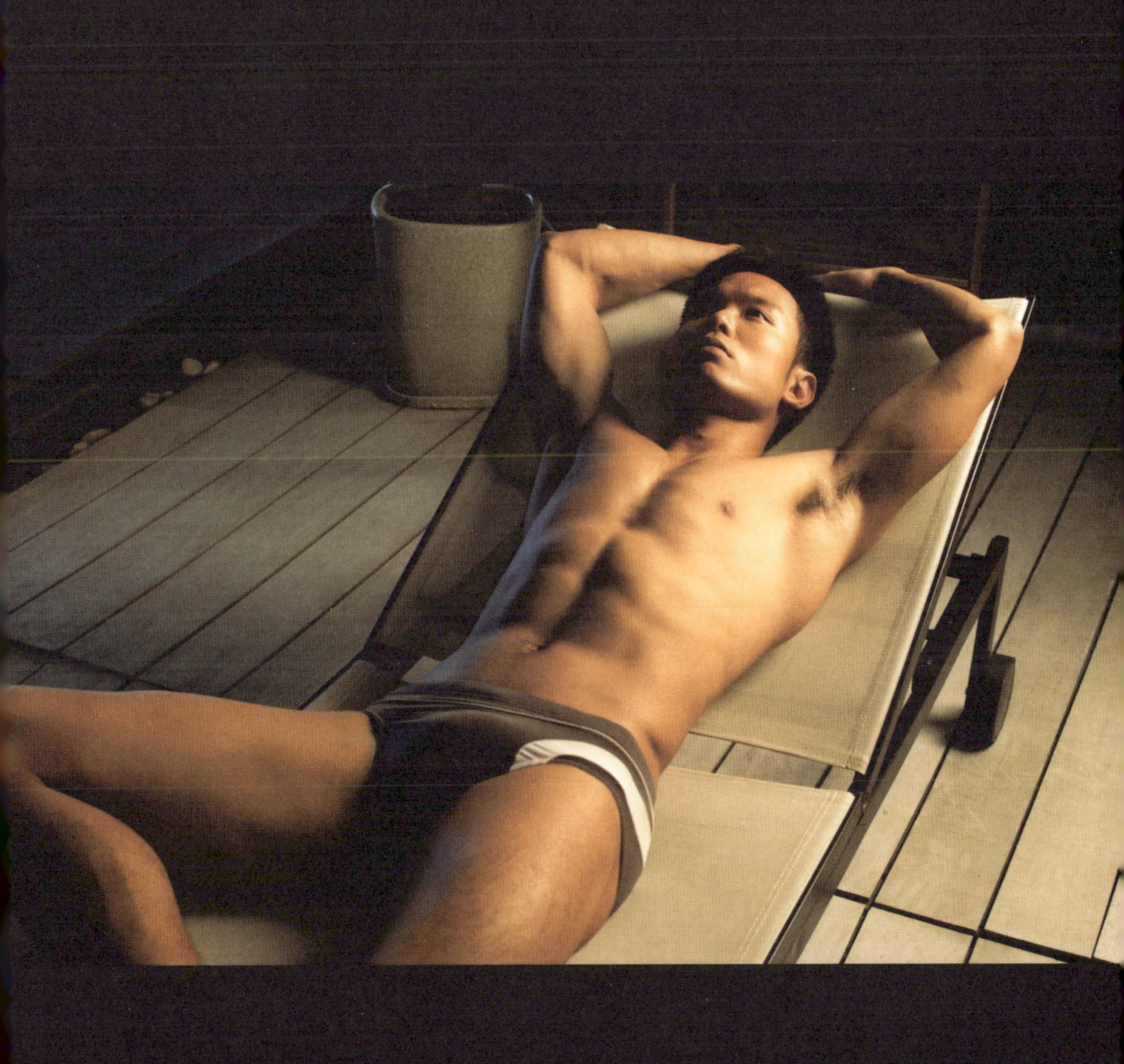

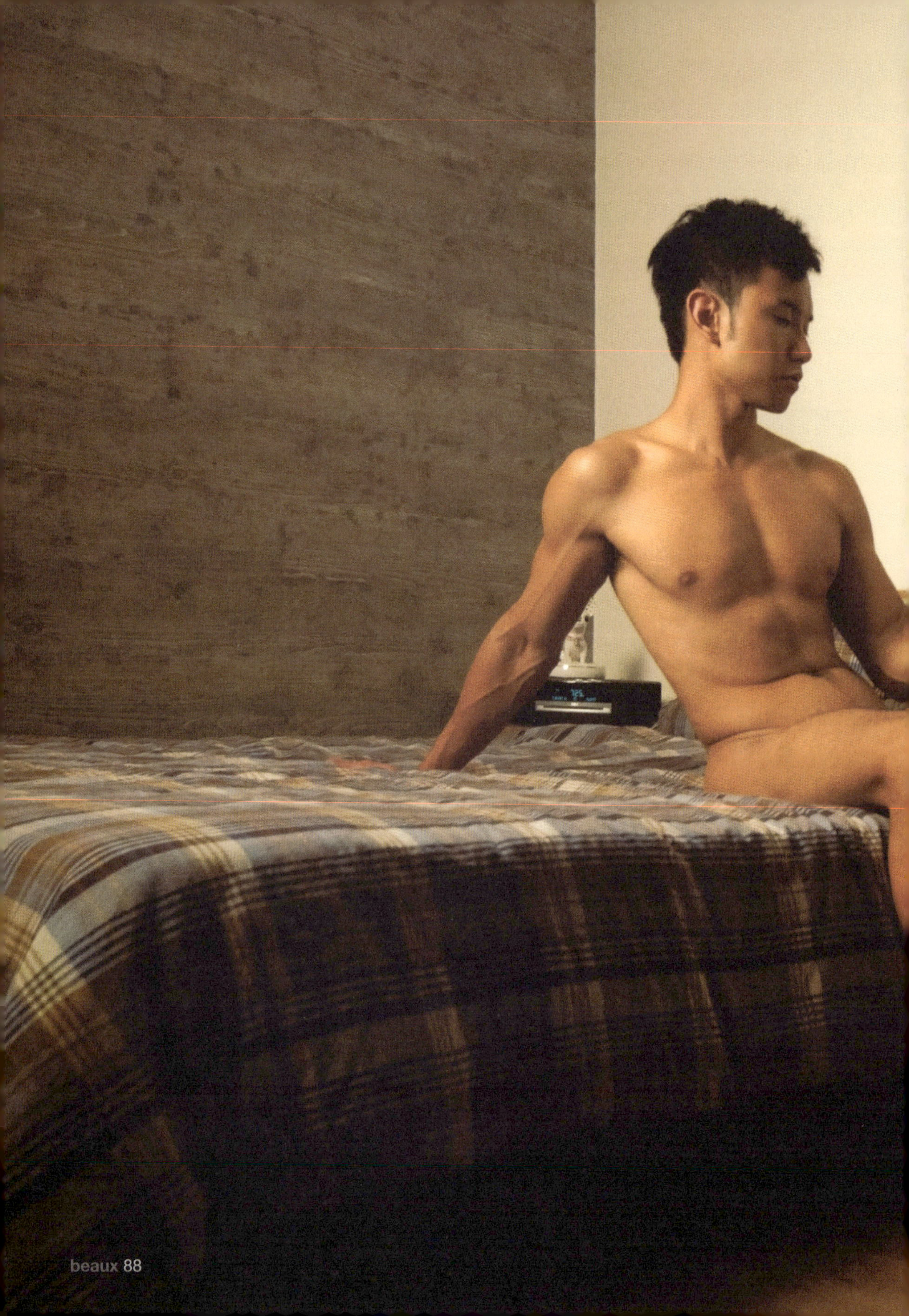

"If there is a single quality that is shared by all great men, it is vanity. But I mean by vanity only that they appreciate their own worth. Without this kind of vanity they would not be great. And with vanity alone, of course, a man is nothing."

Yousef Karsh
Photographer

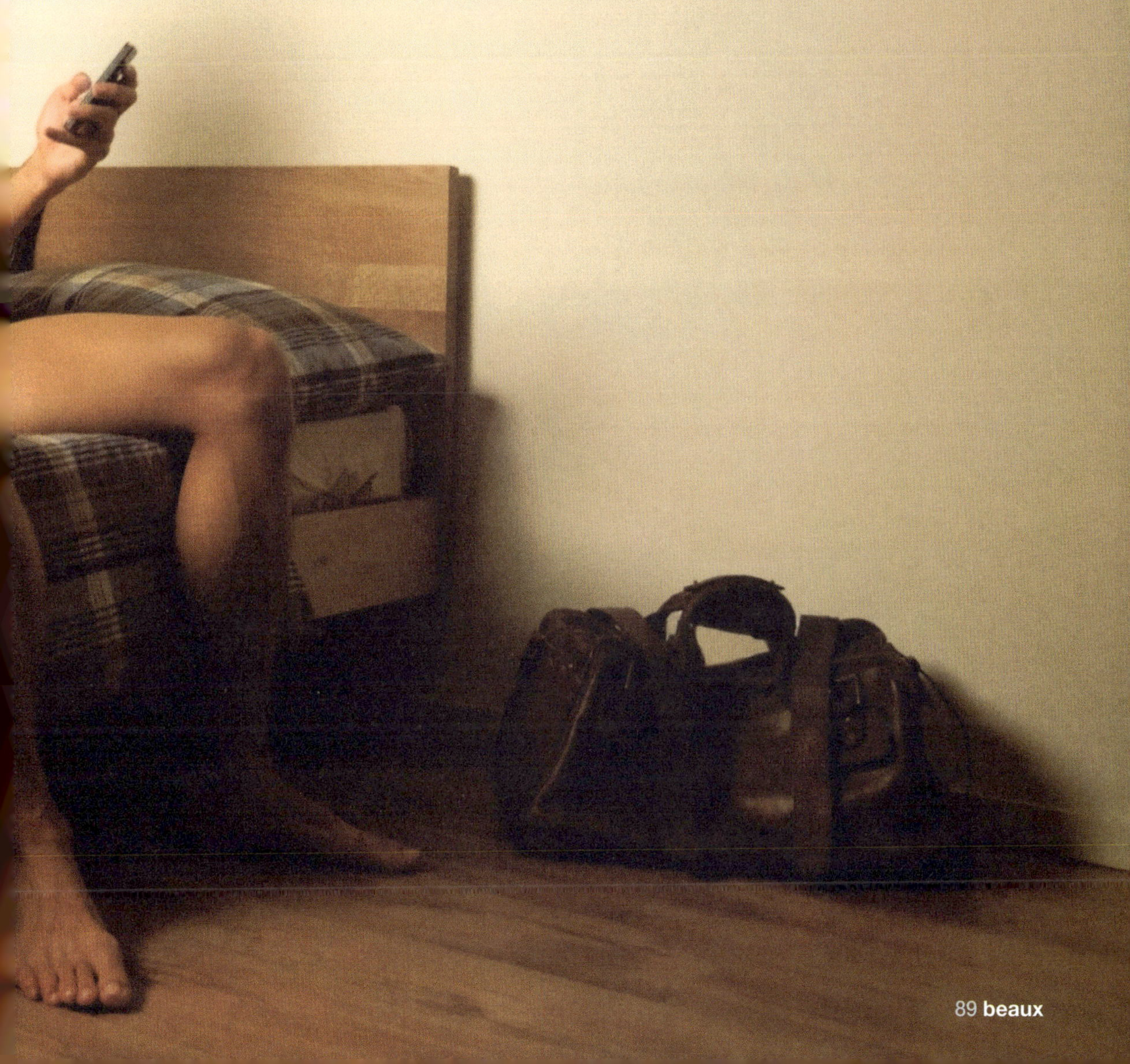

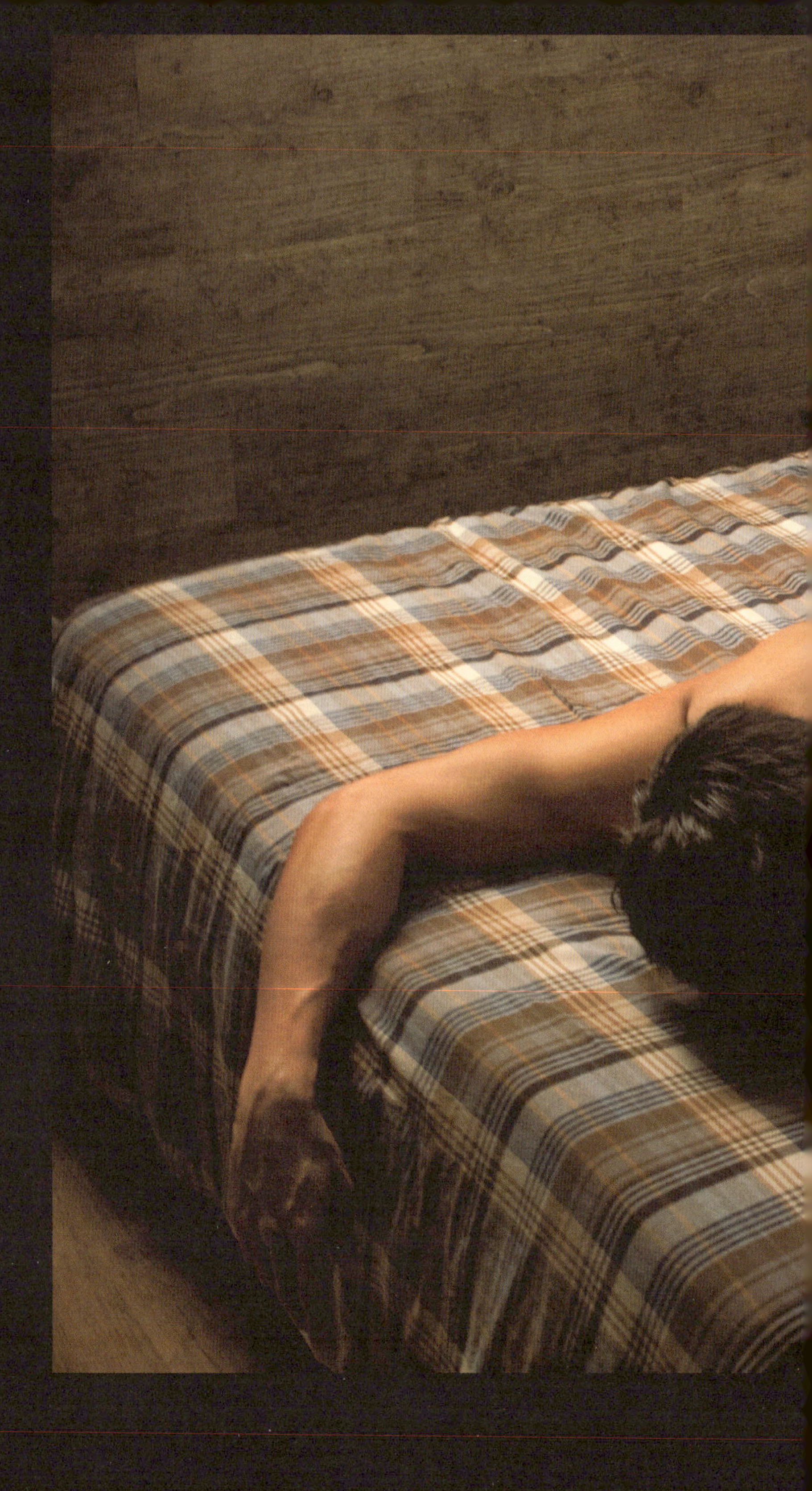

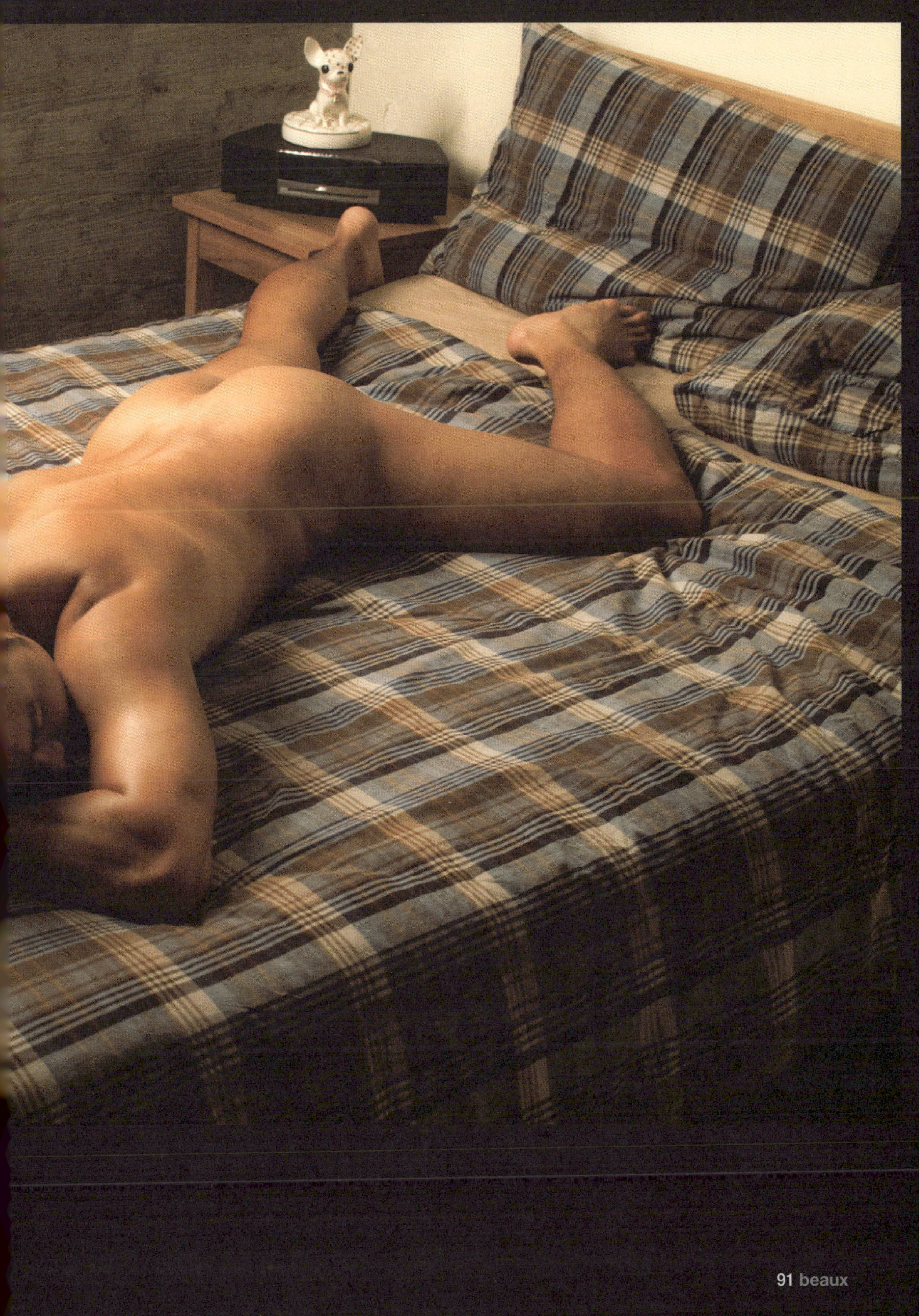

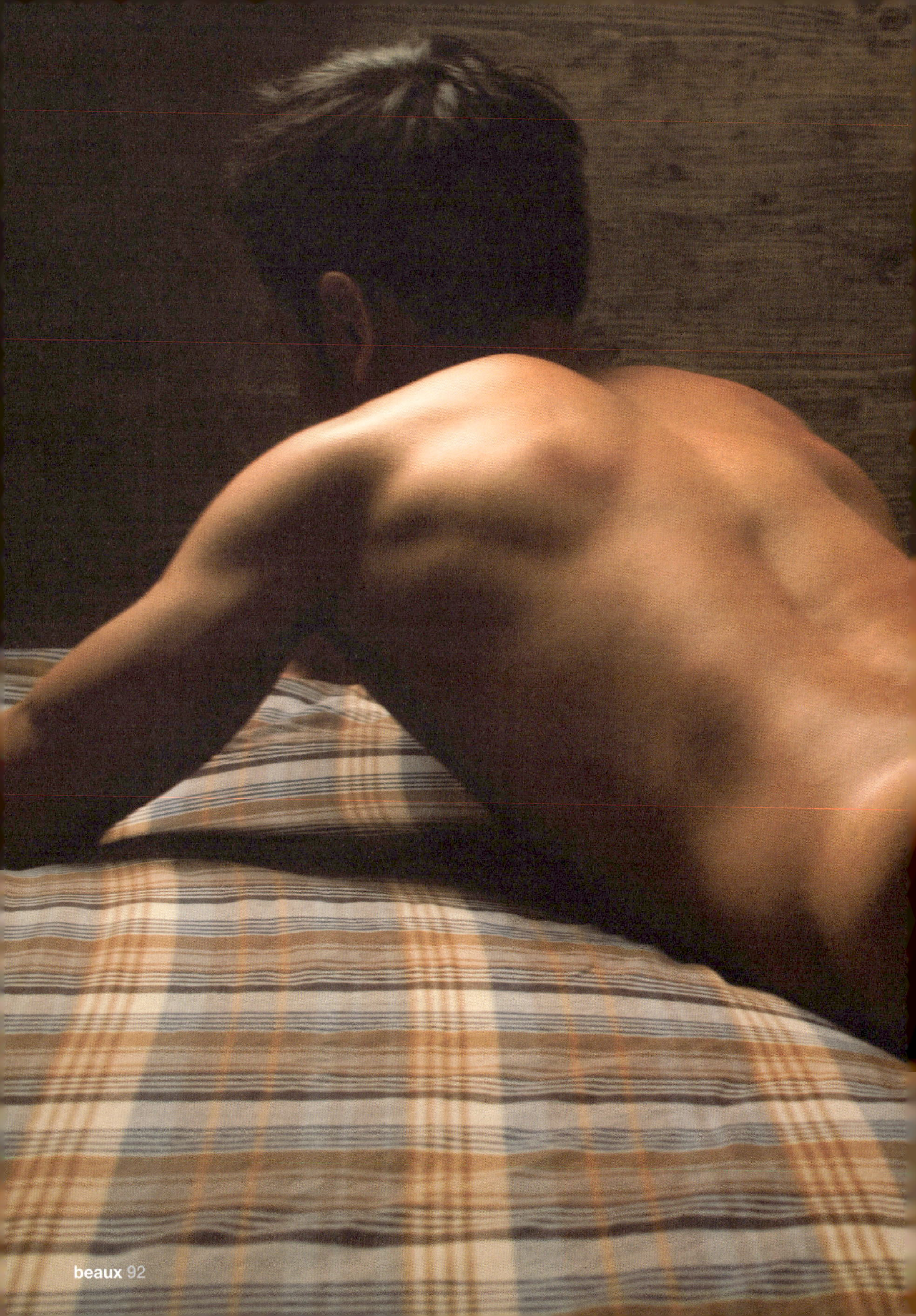

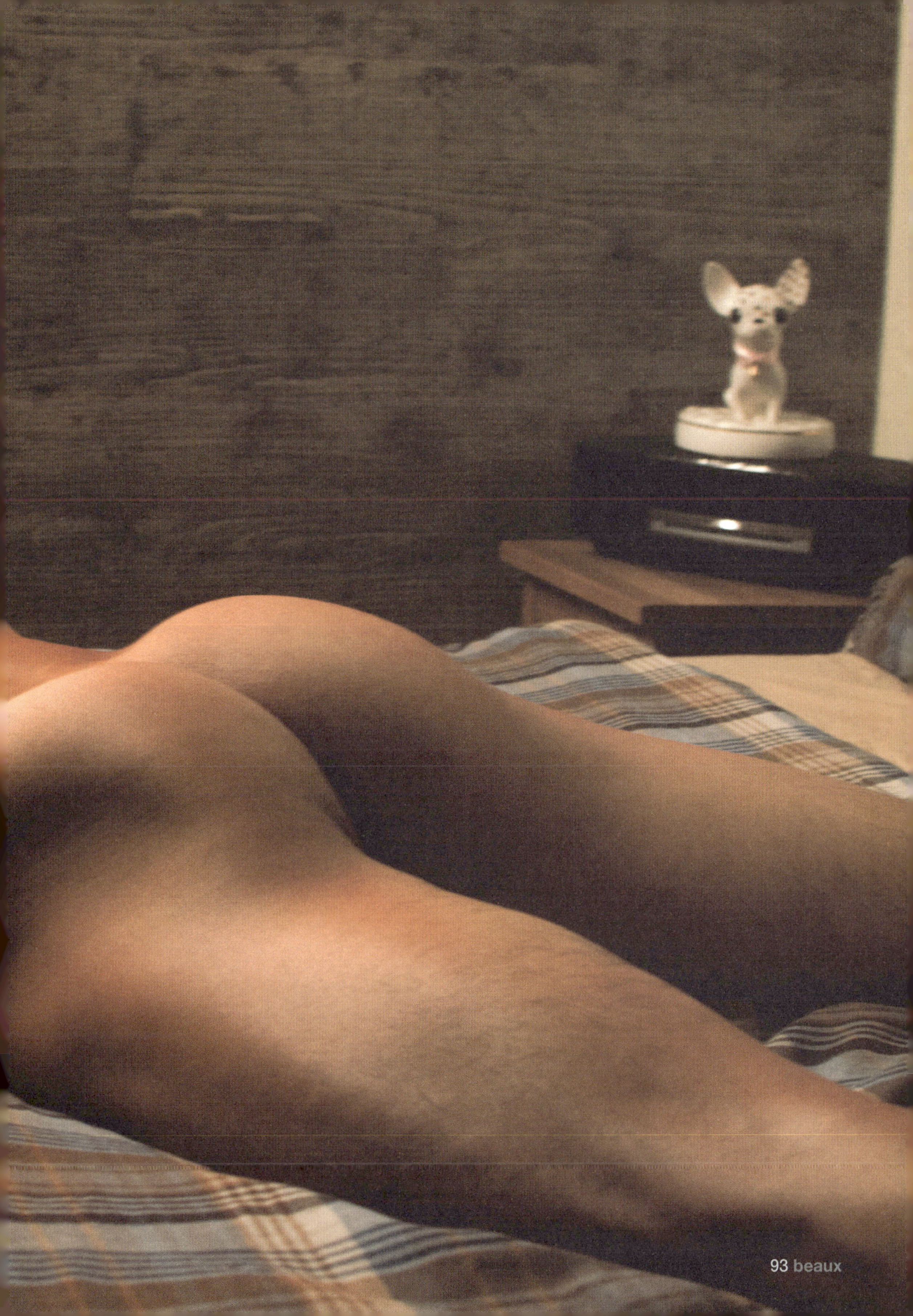

collective

contributors

photographers and individuals

Photographers and individuals are welcome to send in their photographs of Asian men to **submissions@beauxmagazine.com**. All initial photographs must be a minimum of 1200pixels in the length dimension at a minimum of 150dpi. If any images are considered suitable for publication, the final images must be a minimum file size of 3800 x 2500 pixels (or 9 million pixels). While every care is provided to the render the images exactly to the photographer's original image, **beaux** reserves the option to make minor adjustments to the image without permssion to the photographer for overall standard and consistency of **beaux** magazine. All images submitted by contributors shall retain full copyright to the photographs. Photographers must have a model release of submitted images, with the exception of street photography, as showcased in **beauxspotting**. Studio 8 Hong Kong Publishing Ltd. shall not be held responsible for photographer's submissions.

writers

Writers are encouraged to submit articles to **submissions@beauxmagazine.com**. The articles may be fictional or personal in nature, while maintaining relevance to men in general. Alternative topics that will be considered include issues that pertain to gender, sexuality, LGBT, inner and outer beauty, philosophy, vices and victories. It must have a passionate tone that encourage others to become who they are both inside and out.

advertising

Do you want to reach an audience that has higher spending power? Then perhaps **beaux** is exactly what you are looking for. Feel free to contact us at **advertising@beauxmagazine.com** for more information.

beaux team

Founder & Publisher	Norm Yip
Fashion Advisor	Charlie Shingo
Marketing Manager	Jonathan Wu
Sales Agent	Edo Bersma
Photographer	Norm Yip
Editors	Leroy Luar Jefferson Mendoza
Graphics & Layout	Studio 8
Printers	Magnum Printers
Distribution	Hong Kong - Foreign Press International - Bookazine

interested in modeling?

If you have an interest in modeling for **beaux** magazine or for Norm Yip's Asian Male collection, please send 4-5 clear and recent photographs showing your face and body to **submissions@beauxmagazine.com**. Ideally, you should be comfortable being nude or semi-nude in front of a camera and possess both an attractive face and body, besides a friendly and outgoing personality. All potential models are interviewed in person before any final decision is made. We wish you luck and hope to see you in the next issue of **beaux**!

The Asian Male Collection

The Asian Male project started initially as a personal interest, a simple desire to photograph friends of mine from an artistic view. My influences were based on a number of things, including photographer Herb Ritts, my Canadian upbringing on the Saskatchewan prairies, my architectural training, and my quest for beauty in the human body and face.

What I have here in this collection of images are photographs of friends, taken with intention, passion, and love. As an artist, I am always struggling to achieve a perceived perfection, an idealized image that may not be the truth, but only a partial truth. A camera can only view from one angle, from one vantage point. Hence, some models have a 'good side'. As a photographer, I am seeking for that good side in the most truthful way, from my own set of aesthetics.

I owe so much to the models that have allowed me to work with them, to share in the experience, and to entrust me with physical bodies to be photographed nude. In Hong Kong, and for most of Asia, the unadorned body is seen simply as pornography. And only recently, has there been a more normalized acceptance of male beauty. The cosmetic companies and influx of gymnasiums attest to that. Nevertheless, I am extremely indebted to the first few models who believed in me and allowed me to photograph them.

In the end, I want everyone to share in the spirit of photography and the beauty of Asian men from all over.

Norm Yip

To order a signed copy of
The Asian Male - 1.AM or
The Asian Male - 2.AM,
please go to the URL:
http://normyip.com/theasianmale

The Asian Male books are also available through Amazon.com and at selected bookstores.

Coming Soon in 2013
The Asian Male - 3.AM Printed Version
The Asian Male - 1.AM+ iBook version

The Asian Male Website
http://theasianmale.com

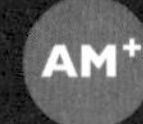

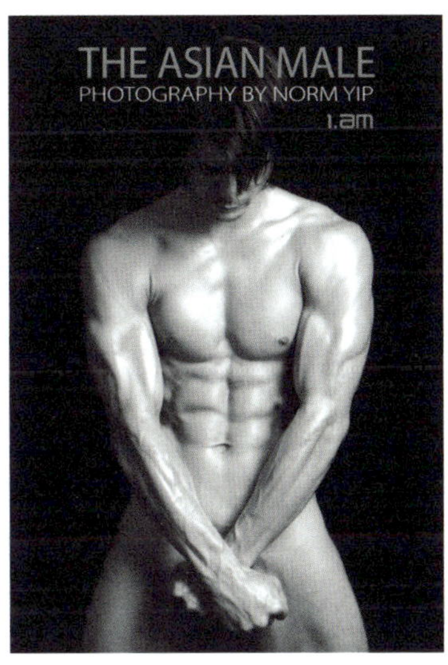

The Asian Male - 1.AM

The Asian Male is Norm Yip s first publication featuring a stunning collection of male images that were taken over a period of five years from 1999 -2004. With models from Korea, Japan, Singapore, Hong Kong and Malaysia, the men that appear in this volume will mark a new beginning to Asian male photography. From the sensuous and erotic to pensive and poetic, Norm captures a mysterious beauty that is beyond the surface. Lean to muscular physiques grace the pages of this inaugural photography book. The book contains 40 selected images in both colour and black and white prints. Measuring 9" x 12" , the book is a hard-cover edition using 250 gsm fine art matt paper stock. Enthusiasts for fine art photography will appreciate the exceptional printing quality of this volume, making this a perfect coffee table book and ideal collector's item.

ISBN 988 98259 1 0

US$44.95

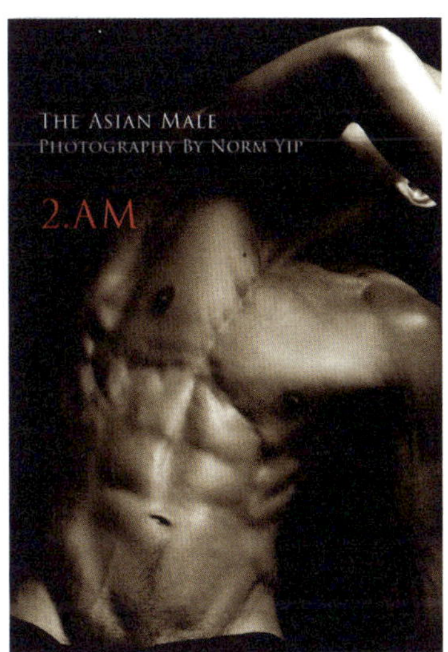

The Asian Male - 2.AM

Speak to any portrait photographer or artist and you will find that at one point in time, the quest for truth, meaning and beauty arises. Norm Yip is one such person on that quest. Through the medium of photography and his passion for the human body and face, he has managed to capture the essence and spirit of Asian men in an unadorned, meaningful fashion. With a keen eye for light and shadow and a preference for black and white photography, Norm stand as one of the Asia's pre-eminent photographers in the field of the fine art male photography. Chinese, Malaysian, Filipino, Japanese, Nepalese and Pakistani men from the world over are featured in *The Asian Male - 2.AM*. From the ripped bodybuilder to the lean and svelte, Yip is able to extract a hidden and mysterious beauty that goes under the skin and beyond the facade.

ISBN 988 98259 2 8

US$44.95

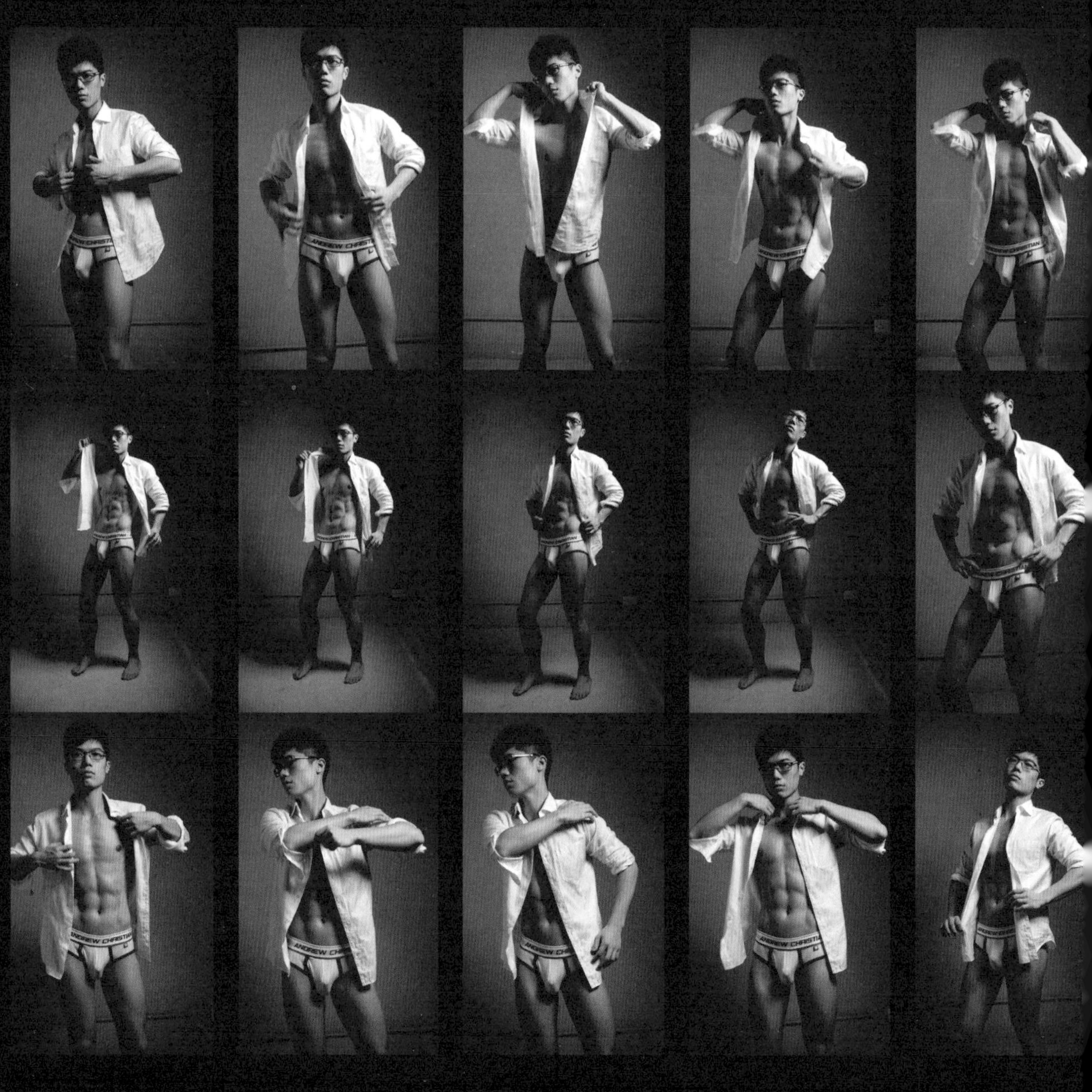
ANDREW CHRISTIAN